Theatre Royal Stratford East pres...

The Big Life

Written by Paul Sirett

Music by Paul Joseph

With an introduction by Philip Hedley,
Artistic Director of Theatre Royal Stratford East

First performed at Theatre Royal Stratford East
Saturday 17 April 2004.

Theatre Royal Stratford East
Gerry Raffles Square
Stratford
London
E15 1BN

www.stratfordeast.com

Theatre Royal
STRATFORD EAST

The Big Life

Book & Lyrics **Paul Sirett**
Music **Paul Joseph**

Cast in alphabetical order

Reverend	**Geoff Aymer**
Mary	**Lorna Brown**
Kathy	**Claudia Cadette**
Mrs Aphrodite	**Tameka Empson**
Zulieka	**Maureen Hibbert**
Jacqueline / Secretary	**Amanda Horlock**
Admiral / Eros	**Jason Pennycooke**
Dennis	**Marcus Powell**
Bernie	**Neil Reidman**
Ferdy	**Victor Romero-Evans**
Lennie	**Chris Tummings**
Sybil	**Yaa**

The Band

Keyboard 1	**Delroy Murray**
Keyboard 2	**Norris Jackson**
Drums	**Perry Melius**
Bass	**Wayne Nunes**
Guitar	**Peter Lee**

Creative team

Director	**Clint Dyer**
Set & Costume Designer	**Jenny Tiramani**
Musical Director for Production	**Robert Hyman**
Musical Director for Performance	**Delroy Murray**
Choreographer	**Jason Pennycooke**
Lighting Designer	**Gerry Jenkinson**
Sound Design	**Gareth Owen**
Deputy Stage Manager on the Book	**Charlie Parkin**
Producer	**Kerry Michael**

Performing at Theatre Royal Stratford East
from 17 April 2004 to 22 May 2004

The Theatre Royal Stratford East's Musical Theatre Journey

Joan Littlewood's company Theatre Workshop arrived at the Theatre Royal Stratford East in 1953 and soon caused a revolution in British theatre, alongside the Royal Court Theatre, principally by giving opportunities to many talented working class writers and actors with the kind of talent previously excluded from theatre.

Among her wide-ranging theatre work there were a handful of musicals which were hailed at one time as the start of a British musical theatre revival. For example in 1963 Joan created *Oh, What A Lovely War!* (right) which was a view of the First World War from the trenches, and which hugely influenced documentary theatre and inspired the

internationally admired Theatre In Education movement, in which Britain lead the world for the next thirty years.

Another example which is significant in the journey that I wish to illustrate here was Lionel Bart's *Fings Ain't Wot They Used T'Be*. Lionel was a raw

talent who couldn't write music down. When the show went to the West End there had to be a two-page glossary of cockney slang in the programme to explain it to the typical West End theatre-goer.

In my own time as artistic director at Theatre Royal since 1979, the West End has cherry-picked our safer compilation shows which used already popular music, such as *Five Guys Named Moe* (left), a tribute to Louis Jordan's music, or *Unforgettable*, a tribute to Nat King Cole, or *A Star Is Torn*, a tribute to eight famous women singers. It also took *The Phantom of the Opera* (below right) and *The Invisible Man* from the extraordinary list of populist shows with music that Ken Hill created at Stratford East.

It must be mentioned that Cameron Mackintosh who transferred *Five Guys Named Moe* to the West End, behaved in an exemplary fashion and offered Stratford East a deal of unheard-of generosity. We received one-third

of his own company's earnings on the show. He simply said we had taken the original risk and so deserved it. Would it was ever thus!

The world-wide profits kept Stratford East going as a lively, risk-taking producing theatre in the early nineties at a time when regional theatres were hard-pushed to keep open let alone take risks. Unfortunately it was only after the *Moe* money had been spent on sheer survival that the Theatre Royal came up with its own 'Big Idea' in 1996 for investing in the research and development process necessary for the creation of a new vein of musical theatre.

The idea was to develop new musicals out of the contemporary music known as Urban Music, which had been popular by 1996 for at least twenty years. The Theatre Royal Stratford East was well-placed to achieve this, with its famous history in musical theatre and its deep roots in its own urban community. This relationship with its local, varied communities has been central to the Theatre Royal's success over the past fifty years. Occasionally it directly produced plays such as *Steaming* which couldn't be more local, set as it was in a local Turkish bath, and yet it went on to the West End, Broadway and Australia and was made into a film.

The last census threw up some startling facts about the Theatre Royal's locality. Newham, in which it is situated, is the borough in Britain with the highest percentage of ethnic minorities who are now in fact a majority – 61% – of the population. It has the highest percentage of young people in its population and the biggest turnover of residents of any borough. It is also one of the most deprived boroughs in the country, a position aggravated by its unaccountable exclusion from being named an inner city borough by the government.

These factors combined allow Newham to claim to be on the front-line of social change. It also happens that if any area in Britain can claim to be the cradle of UK hip-hop music, then it is the East End. The Theatre Royal read the writing on the wall and so eight years ago began a process of developing the Urban Musical, while not excluding or disparaging the creation of new musicals in the classic Broadway tradition.

The genre now called Urban Music represents an extraordinary range of musical forms which are continually evolving and fusing. These include R'n'B, hip-hop, rap, basement, garage and bashment among other forms. Like so much of popular music its roots are in black culture. However with the rich mix of races in Britain's inner cities, culturally diverse fusions of musical styles are inevitably happening, notably with Asian music, from which not just populist forms like Bhangra and Bollywood are appropriated to add to the mix but also elements of Indian classical music. The fusions possible in Urban Music have no boundaries.

It is greatly to the advantage of the originality of British pop music that this mixing of styles of music from different racial backgrounds happens more readily in London than in, say, New York. There is the advantage too that no country has the particular mix of cultures that Britain has from its colonial history, and so the contemporary musicals developed in Britain will by definition be different to those developed in the USA.

An exciting fusion of culturally diverse talents has contributed much to the British pop music and club music scenes and to the distinctive British successes in the worlds of fashion and film. In the performing arts, contemporary dance has been inspired by new musical fusions, but the world of theatre has remained largely untouched by them.

Right here, though, I must acknowledge the most significant British predecessor to the Theatre Royal's Musical Theatre Project. Armani Napthali showed with his explosive production *Ragamuffin* (whose script is published by Oberon Books) just how effectively rap and hip-hop could be used to tell a complex political story. This production toured briefly to Stratford East in the early nineties and I'd like to believe, had I seen it then, it would have pointed me towards our own project earlier.

I'm very glad, though, that Armani re-staged it in our re-opening season in 2002, along with Jonzi D's remarkable, dance-based, hip-hop show *Aeroplane Man*, and that the Theatre Royal was thus able to pay homage to two formidably talented pioneers early in its own journey on the same road.

When the Theatre Royal began its research-and-development process into using British Urban Music in musicals, we were told by two leading West End producers that this wasn't possible to do because it simply wasn't 'musical theatre music'. The same was said early last century about ragtime, then later about jazz and yet again about rock and roll. There was always a delay between these musical forms coming through in popular music and finally being imported into musical theatre. There was for example a fourteen-year gap between rock and roll dominating the hit parade in 1955 and the staging of the first successful rock musical *Hair* in 1968.

However there has now been a twenty-five year lag between the rise of rap and hip-hop in the pop charts and the staging of a UK Urban musical on the West End stage, which seems to indicate a serious problem for the future popularity of the musical as an art form.

Why is this? It's partly the usual historical reasons. Powerful commercial producers tend to be middle-aged, white males who don't connect with the new music. Their audiences tend to be over forty, partly because only by that age can many afford West End prices, and those audiences are often nostalgic for the music of their youth.

However there are particular reasons why the new Urban Music has taken longer to be accepted in theatre. One is that, unlike traditional musicals, which depend on a combination of live musicians, technology is central to the new music. So there has to be a major re-think and much experimentation for creating a new musical theatre, but one which will probably be as dependent as ever on the eternal dramatic verities of character creation and good story-telling.

Perhaps more important at this early stage of development though would be the fact that there are comparatively few black and Asian writers and composers concentrating on musical theatre, partly because they can see so few role models to encourage them to do so. Noticeably none of the famous musical writing teams in the USA in the last century were black, although the original sources of the new American popular music were primarily black and to a lesser extent Jewish.

With all these issues in mind, Theatre Royal Stratford East began in 1999 a series of annual, month-long, full-time workshops to experiment in using all manner of contemporary popular music in theatre. The participants included playwrights who had already worked in theatre but were interested in writing the book and/or lyrics for a musical. Most of the composers involved had never worked in musical theatre before. They worked in many different musical traditions but there was gradually year by year a greater concentration on contemporary Urban Music because it became obvious that was the most difficult and possibly the most productive style of music to incorporate into musicals. As one of the West End producers who thought the task was impossible added, 'but if you crack it you'll make a fortune'.

The courses are lead by two lecturers, Fred Carl and Robert Lee, from the Tisch School at New York University, which has the only university course in the world which teaches the art of writing for musical theatre. It's a two-year, post-graduate course and it is very expensive to do and of course to live in New York. Hardly any of those doing Stratford East's month-long courses would be academically qualified enough or rich enough to do the New York two-year course. The young Lionel Bart would have been neither, for example. The lecturers concerned are excited by the diversity in age, race and experience of the participants we find for them and they say there is no equivalent producing theatre in New York concentrating on developing contemporary urban musicals as Stratford East is.

After six years, over one hundred writers and composers have taken part in Stratford East's extremely practical courses. Approximately 60% of them have been black with 20% Asian and 20% white.

Progressing artists from these annual July Musical Theatre Workshops can be a painstaking and expensive business. An excellent example of a composing and writing team developed from the first July Workshop are the poet Hope Massiah and the composer Delroy Murray, who went on to the second stage of workshopping, for which they were commissioned to write a 20 minute show. It was staged by a director in studio circumstances enabling them to see professional actors and musicians performing their work for the first time.

This was followed up with a commission to write an eighty-minute show, *One Dance Will Do*, which toured the East End, and finally they became the first black, words-and-music team to write a traditional British pantomime, but with a Caribbean and Urban Music flavour. Their *Jack and the Beanstalk* was enthusiastically received by the Stratford East audience, which is the most multi-racial of any in British theatre. Stratford East has now commissioned this team to write an original musical and another pantomime. As so often in the ideal plan for the development of a team, Hope and Delroy have been guided by an experienced director, in this case our deputy artistic director, Kerry Michael.

Since the Theatre Royal re-opened in December 2001, it has only been able to afford three new large-scale musicals, to bring to fulfilment the work of other artists we want to develop from our workshops. The first was the extraordinary *Baiju Bawra* (left), with music by Niraj Chag, a twenty-four year old graduate of the first July workshop.

The music was a fusion of Indian classical music with contemporary beats and sampling. When Niraj was asked in an interview with the BBC what was the source of the music, as a very serious question, he replied, 'Well it came from my council-house home really. My mother was into classical music, my father was into Bollywood and my brother into Britpop. So I grew up with all of that, and fused it.' This is typical of the influences on young people today.

The show was directed and designed by the international director/designer ULTZ who is a long-term member of the Theatre Royal's Musical Theatre Committee, which met regularly, until the theatre could no longer afford the modest honorariums involved. The show provoked passionate partisan comment, for and against.

The most radical and significant example to date of what Stratford East is trying to achieve is the production it staged in May 2003 called *Da Boyz* (right). It was a modern version of the 1930's Broadway show *The Boys from Syracuse* by Rodgers and Hart. It was the first time that permission had been given to update the music of a classic

Broadway show still in copyright. This exciting opportunity came about because the enterprising Rodgers and Hammerstein Organisation recognised the high seriousness with which Stratford East was approaching the process. This was a coup for British Theatre.

The music was updated by two young East Enders of nineteen and twenty-two, DJ Excalibah and MC Skolla, and directed and designed by ULTZ who conceived the whole idea. The main aim of Stratford East's Urban Musical Theatre project was to connect with young people who wouldn't normally go to the theatre. This show did that highly successfully because it was their music and because it was set in the East End today. The cast were principally rappers and hip-hoppers drawn from auditions throughout the East End, and many were graduates of the Theatre Royal's Youth Theatres. The young people were in effect the style gurus and everything was done to make young people feel they owned the show.

Techniques for marketing were drawn, with EMI's advice, from how the commercial music business connected with young people, and this had excellent results. Young offenders teams, mentoring groups and youth clubs from tough areas booked young people in and many of them re-booked to come again individually, breaking that invisible but daunting barrier many young people feel exists between them and theatre. To add to this remarkable local and social achievement, the show was internationally and artistically acknowledged with a whole page report in the New York Times and another whole page in the American entertainment bible 'Variety' hailing it as a 'break-through in international music theatre' and calling the Theatre Royal a 'pioneering theatre'.

The third in the trio of musicals which have so far grown out of the July Musical Theatre Workshops and been staged at the Theatre Royal is *The Big Life*, the script and lyrics of which are published in this book by the ever-adventurous Oberon Books.

The idea for the show came from Paul Sirett who had had three plays staged at the Theatre Royal in the early nineties. The Theatre Royal linked him up with composer Paul Joseph, who had done the first of the July workshops, and with director Clint Dyer who had worked on our whole musical theatre enterprise from the very beginning.

This show is not of course a contemporary urban musical, but interestingly it has a form of street music, ska, which has been neglected by musical theatre. Ska is the immediate predecessor of reggae, which in turn contributed much to hip-hop. The belief of course is that the music and subject matter will connect directly with older generations who remember the fifties or the ska revival of the early eighties, and the hope is too that the music will build a bridge to young people who will recognise elements of their own music in ska.

To connect theatre with young people the Theatre Royal's Education Department always has a series of classroom activities and workshops for schools associated with its major productions. Just how integrated these activities are with the professional theatre work is exemplified in the project where graduates from our July Musical Theatre workshops went into schools to work with students creating their own 20-minute musicals, which were then performed on the Theatre Royal's stage. Paul Joseph, composer of *The Big Life*, is doing sessions in schools on ska. A good example of how the circle can be completed between our education work and our stage can be seen in the fact that Clint Dyer, was first emboldened to join our Youth Theatre by a visit of Theatre Royal actors to his school twenty-one years ago, and now he is directing *The Big Life*, and is a board member of the Theatre Royal.

The Theatre Royal is not alone in its epic journey to bring a new impetus to British musical theatre and to involve a new generation in theatre indirectly. Feeding the process are all manner of grass-roots organisations, sometimes labelled Youth Arts, which in a huge variety of ways, either founded their existence on Urban Music or they use it as the most accessible bridge into other art forms, or to bring disaffected young people back into society and even formal education, or to lead them into careers in the music industry. With the current government's huge concern about social inclusion and about equipping young people with skills, it could well look favourably at increased investment in the Youth Arts world.

There is also a well-respected, black, touring theatre company called NITRO which is investing in the development of new urban musicals. However there is no building-based theatre like the Theatre Royal which has devoted so much time, energy and money to developing the whole process from education work, through to a large-scale training programme for artists, through to workshopping, commissioning and finally the staging of the musicals.

This whole process costs a very great deal of money. One of the only good things about the destructive, constantly extended, closed period for refurbishment the Theatre Royal Stratford East suffered (which finally covered the four years from 1998 to 2001 inclusively) was that it was able to concentrate on its musical theatre project during that time. The funders of our core operation, the borough of Newham, the Association of London Government and the Arts Council of England, continued their support in the closed period. Upon re-opening the Theatre Royal met the financial crisis which most arts organisations experienced after a closure for Lottery-financed refurbishing, with the Theatre Royal having more excuse than any other organisation since its closure period was extended longer than anybody's.

I tell this tale here because Stratford East's Musical Theatre Project is fighting for survival. In response to the apparently inevitable financial crisis upon re-opening, the Arts Council England rescued the Theatre Royal and is still backing it to go through a process called Recovery for its continued existence. The bridging money offered though was not sufficient to enable the Theatre Royal to continue its musical theatre research-and-development at full flood. Some damaging cuts had to be made and the staging of *The Big Life* delayed twice.

The Theatre Royal will unquestionably battle through to keep its Musical Theatre Project alive and to benefit from the visible rewards ahead which are encouraging us to keep going.

Already we have been supported in our seven years of development by an extraordinarily varied number of organisations which can see the theatrical, social and educational benefits of the project. Just look at this list of unlikely bed-fellows: The Esmée Fairbairn Foundation, The Follett Foundation, The Hollick Foundation, The Gulbenkian Foundation, The Unity Theatre Trust, The Equity Trust, The Cameron Mackintosh Foundation and the TUC. To add to the mixture we have indications too of future support from the Financial Services Authority and UBS. Senior employees at UBS, a leading financial services firm in the City, have also begun to provide business and management advice to staff at the theatre.

There are straws in the wind too that give indications of possible future commercial success. Prior to the closure period the Theatre Royal's main aim of staging new, often ground-breaking, populist shows to entertain its local communities, produced on average one show every two years that transferred to the West End. Since re-opening there has been little West End interest in Stratford East's mainly black and often musical output.

However there has been a new, marked interest from British and US film and TV companies. There have been suggestions of filming *Da Boyz* and even of re-staging one of our black revues, *Funny Black Women on the Edge*, in a Harlem theatre to be filmed there. Discussions are still continuing, and there have been too many of these expressions of interest from the mechanical media, for it not to be the signal of new opportunities ahead for Stratford East's work. It is fascinating that it is a theatre which is so closely involved with its local community that is getting these international inquiries.

The Theatre Royal's Musical Theatre Project has the potential too to build bridges between education and theatre.

Many Youth Arts organisations have already seen that rap and hip-hop can be of great service to the educational world, not least because rap has lead young people back to an interest in lyrics, and therefore literacy, which rock-and-roll did not. Now the Gulbenkian Foundation has given the Theatre Royal a grant to explore the feasibility of developing a package for schools to enable them to create, as the Theatre Royal did, musically up-dated versions of *The Boys from Syracuse*, which has its roots in Shakespeare and classical Greek comedy. So there will be a show available for a school's annual musical production, which connects directly with young people's current musical interest, which no established musical currently does.

Already some local schools are interested in *The Big Life* as a potential for study in five different subjects, drama, dance, music, history and citizenship.

All organisations these days seem to be striving for 'joined-up thinking', both internally and with other organisations in other spheres of interest. The Theatre Royal can boast it has been practising joined-up thinking internally and between theatre arts, community, training and education for fifty years. The massive changes facing the East End are now compelling it to look to creating new relationships of hugely varied kinds.

The Theatre Royal is now surrounded by more physical developments than any other producing-theatre in Europe. It's at the heart of the Thames Gateway, in itself the biggest development project in Europe, which will bring a town the size of Leeds into the area between the City, and the sea. Add to that the arrival of the Euro-train station and dwellings for 30,000 people, both being built across the road from the theatre. Then there's the Olympic bid, which if successful would mean the main stadium would be ten minutes' walk away.

Innumerable quangos, committees and pressure groups are searching for the Big Idea to get culture effectively onto the agendas of the Thames Gateway and the Olympic bid. Stratford East believes it has the nub of that idea in its Musical Theatre Project. By definition the Olympics are young and multi-cultural. So is Stratford East's idea, and it links up aptly with a whole string of organisations and educational institutions throughout the East End.

Musical Theatre is the most collaborative popular art form. So it links, for example, with the three resident organisations next door at Stratford Circus, which happen to centre on dance, music and theatre, i.e. East London Dance, Urban Development and Theatre Venture. It also links with NewVic which may play a bigger role in the Circus in the future and which had a huge increase in its number of performing arts students in recent years.

Then there's the extraordinary, wide-ranging music organisation, Ocean, in Hackney opposite the gloriously restored Hackney Empire. In Tower Hamlets there's the soon-to-be-established, equally wide-ranging and ambitious Rich Mix venture. The growing investment of innumerable educational institutions into the performing arts throughout the East End is epitomised by Hackney Council and UBS combining to establish a new Academy school centring on Maths and Music.

The Theatre Royal is pursuing partnerships with all the above arts organisations and many more. It needs to develop new relationships with commercial organisations, developers, government bodies and quangos. It knows it has a great deal to offer them and all of the new East End.

It is keenly aware that it only needs partners who can see that, while it is enthusiastically open to change, it must maintain its values as a risk-taking, guerrilla theatre which keeps in close touch with its community, and young people. Damage that process and you kill the goose that has laid many golden eggs in its time. Preserve it and all those who join us in our musical theatre enterprise will find some great rewards.

Philip Hedley
Artistic Director
Theatre Royal Stratford East
phedley@stratfordeast.com

Cast in Alphabetical Order

Geoff Aymer Reverend

Geoff is an actor / writer / comedian. His acting work includes such productions as *A Yorkshire Tragedy* (Royal Court Theatre Upstairs); *The Wiz* (Hackney Empire); a comedy version of *Macbeth* (Young Vic); and Pirandello's *Henry IV* in which he played the central character. As a comedian, he was formerly one half of double act *Aymer and Powell* whose highlight was an appearance on BBC 2's *The Real McCoy*. As a solo artist, he is most noted for his alter ego, *'Sexy' Rex Carmichael*. Other TV credits include: *The A Force* (BBC2) and *Club Class* (Channel Five).

His playwriting credits include *Got Your Number*, *What A Wonderful World*, and most notably, *The Oddest Couple* which was written for Robbie Gee and Eddie Nestor, and was staged here at the Theatre Royal in February.

Lorna Brown Mary

Theatre credits include: *Da Boyz*, *Funny Black Women on the Edge*, *Shoot2 Win*, *One Dance Will Do*, *Zumbi* (Stratford East); *The Hommage Behind* (LSW); *Itsy Bitsy Spider* (Talawa); *Up Against the Wall* (Tricycle); *Othello* (*New Victoria Theatre in Stoke*). Previous theatre credits include originating the role of 'Timoune' in *Once on This Island* for the Birmingham Rep and in the West End, *King at the Piccadilly*; *Mass Carib* at the Albany and *Beulah's Box* on tour.

TV and Film includes: *Family Business*, *Holby City*, *Rough Treatment*, *Bad Girls*, *Murder Most Horrid*, *Dangerfield*, *The Bill*, *Casualty*, *Anna Lee*, and *It Happened to Me*.

Lorna has sung with *The Kiss of Life* and in 1997 supported *Gladys Knight* on tour. She has also performed with Courtney Pine and The Jazz Warriors. She is currently writing and performing her own songs.

Claudia Cadette Kathy

Claudia graduated from the Italia Conti Academy in London, whilst making her first professional appearance in *Miss Saigon* (Theatre Royal, Drury Lane). She then went on to play 'Young Dinah' in *The Cotton Club* (Aldwych Theatre); *A Tribute to Sammy Davis Jnr* (Theatre Royal Drury Lane); 'Chiffon' in *Little Shop of Horrors* (Derby Playhouse); the title role of 'Josephine Baker' in the musical *Bakerfix* (Germany, directed by Clarke Peters); 'Laura' in *Sweet Lorraine* (National UK tour); 'Armelia' in *Ain't Misbehavin'* (Perth Theatre); 'Debbie & Ugly Sister' in *Heavenly Bodies* and

Sondheim's *Into the Woods* (Leicester Haymarket); *Dancing and Singing the Blues* (European tour); 'Althea Leyton' in *Snakehips* by Clarke Peters (The National Theatre); Original London cast of *Rent* (Shaftesbury Theatre); *Troilus & Cressida*, *Darker Face* and *Candide* (The National Theatre); 'Pamela' in *Poison* (Tricycle Theatre); 'Devil Narrator' in *Millenium Mysteries* (Belgrade/Teatr Biuro Podrozy); the title role of 'Aladdin' in *Aladdin* (Oxford Playhouse). She recently shot the Independent feature *Into Swans*.
Television credits include: 'Beverley Hodge' in *Family Affairs* (Channel 5); 'Rhetta Kirkpatrick' in *Holby City* (BBC); *Gimme Gimme Gimme* (BBC).
Cast Recordings: *Miss Saigon* and *Candide* (First Night Records).

Tameka Empson Mrs Aphrodite

Tameka Empson trained at the Anna Scher Theatre School. Her theatre credits include: *Our House* (Cambridge Theatre, West End), *Top Girls*, *Splash Hatch On The E*, *Girls On Top*, *Going Down* (Donmar Warehouse), *Inkle and Yarico* (B.A.C), *Cockroach Who and Bondage* (Royal Court) and *Shalom Soweto* performed at the Anna Scher Theatre and directed by Anna Scher.
Tameka has made numerous appearances on television including: *Three Non Blondes* (Brown Eyed Boy/BBC), *Babyfather*, *Thinkabout, Arena: The Beano & The Dandy, Desperate to Act, A Taste for Death* and *Eastenders* for the BBC.

She has also starred in *Sam's Game* (ITV) and *London's Burning (LWT)*. Film credits include: *Beautiful Thing* (World Productions), *Prince of Denmark Hill* (Crucial Films), *I Want You* directed by Michael Winterbottom and *Food of Love* directed by Stephen Poliakoff.

Maureen Hibbert Zulieka

Maureen's studies in African, Caribbean Dance & Cultural Studies-Irie Theatre/Birbeck College and a BA from Middlesex University – formed a platform for a career predominately in theatre, beginning with *Dreams of Innana: Pan Project* (Central & Southern India).
Since *Ragamuffin*; produced by Creative Origins and UK Arts International last came to Theatre Royal, Maureen has performed as a ska dancer in *Wondrous Oblivion* (APT Films); *State of Play* (Endor Productions) and filmed in Croatia on *The Fever* (FeverShawn Productions).
Other credits include: *The Crucible* (Abbey Theatre, Dublin); *The Coup* (The National Theatre); *A Jamaican Airman Forsees His Death* (Royal Court Theatre); *Stamping, Shouting & Singing Home* (Birmingham Rep) and *Cut and Trust* (TRSE).

Films include: *Notting Hill* (Bookshop Productions); *The Sculptress* (Red Rooster); *Budha of Surburbia*, *The Real McCoy* (BBC) and reliving 50's London in *Head over Heels* (Carnival Films).
Voiceover: *Hardware* (Picture Palace) and Radio, *Like That*.
Vocals: *Ad Infinite:The Revolution Will Not Be Televised* (Genaside II/Durban Poison Records).

Amanda Horlock Jacqueline / Secretary

Amanda grew up in Stratford and attended the youth theatre here at the Theatre Royal as a teenager and first appeared here in *A Class of our Own* in the 80's. Recent theatre includes: *As You Like It*, *Troilus & Cressida*, *Huckleberry Finn and Woyzek* (at the award winning Tobacco Factory Theatre in Bristol); *The Invisible Man* and *'Cleo Camping Emanuelle & Dick* playing Barbara Windsor (Oldham Coliseum); *Dick Whittington* (Nottingham Playhouse); *She Stoops to Conquer* (Northcott Theatre, Exeter) and *Once a Catholic* in Leatherhead and tour. TV credits include: *Hystoryonic* (*Robin Hood, Mary Queen of Scots*), currently showing, *The Debt, Over Here and The Prostitutes' Padre* (BBC). *A Touch of Frost* (Yorkshire TV) and *Innocents* (HTV).
Radio: *The Element of Water, Ferrara Journal* and *A Gothic Quest* all for Radio 4. Amanda has trained in Commedia dell'Arte mask theatre in Italy with Antonio Fava. She also performs her own solo show – *Advice To a Daughter*. This is Amanda's first professional appearance at Theatre Royal Stratford East.

Jason Pennycooke Choreographer – Admiral / Eros

Jason has trained at NSCD, London Studio Centre. His theatre credits include: *Sammy* (Theatre Royal Stratford East); *CATS* (UK tour); *Five Guys Named Moe* (UK tour, Albery Theatre); *Starlight Express* (West End); *Hey Mr Producer* (Lyceum); *Soul Train* (WestEnd); *Elegies* (Globe Theatre); *Rent* (UK tour, West End); *White Folks* (Tricycle); *Golden Boy* (Greenwich); *Simply Heavenly* (Young Vic) and *Stomp* (West End).
Jason's film credits include: *Shopping* (Jude Law); *Stay Lucky* (YTV). He has also appeared in commercials for British Fashion Awards and DeBeers. His video credits include: *Eternal Video* (Good Thing), *Toni Braxton* (Why Did an Angel); *Moorcheeba* (One Fine Day); *Spice World Tour*, *Mel B* (Tell Me & I Want you Back); *M.J Day* (Michael Jackson). Other credits include: *VW Trade Show* (MTV Germany) and *Live and Kicking* (ITV).

Jason has appeared in adverts for Coca-Cola, Halifax, Chupa Chups, Ford Focus, Clarks, Idents for Dreem Team and the Millenium Dome.

Choreography credits: *Red Riding Hood* and *Sammy* (Theatre Royal Stratford East); Mel B (I Want U Back); Fox Kids advert (Cable); Vidal Sassoon (World); M.J. Day (London); UK Garage Awards (2000 & 2001); *Fame Academy* (Endemol) and *Poison Arrow* (Independent).

Teaching credits: LSC Dance Theatre Of Harlem.

Dedicated to the memory of his mother.

Marcus Powell Dennis

Marcus Powell has appeared in numerous theatre productions including: *The Baptism and the Toilet* (Civic Arts Centre); *In the Ruins* (Bristol Old Vic); *A Rock in Water* and *A Yorkshire Tragedy* (both Royal Court Theatre Upstairs).

His theatre writing credits include: *Night of the Dons 2 –The Big Payback* (Theatre Royal Stratford East); *The Thing about Shirley* (Bullion Room Theatre); *Incompatibly Yours* (National Black Theatre Festival USA and Lyric Theatre, Hammersmith) and the record breaking *Independent Black Woman* (Hackney Empire).

His TV, film and radio writing/performing credits include: *The A Force* (BBC), *Kerching!* (CBBC); *A Night with the Kings* (TMW Productions); *Single Voices* (Carlton TV) for which he received a 'Best TV Actor' nomination at the EMMA awards 2001) and *A Blaggers Guide to Black History* (Channel 4), which won the Best TV entertainment prize at The R.I.M.A ceremony 2000 and the BBC Radio 4 sitcom *Do Nothing 'Til You Hear From Me.*

Neil Reidman Bernie

Born in Birmingham of Jamaican parentage. Theatre credits include: *Ticket to Write, Two Tracks and Text Me* (West Yorkshire Playhouse); *Fruit Salad* (Greenwich Theatre); *The Blacks* (Young Vic Studio); *Angels in America* (Library Theatre, Manchester); *The Dispute* (RSC/The Lyric, Hammersmith, European tour and Winner of TMA Best Touring Production, 1999); *Playland, The Dutchman, Merchant of Venice, Pinocchio* (Birmingham Repertory Theatre); *Zumbi* (Black Theatre Co-Op, Theatre Royal Stratford East) and *Too Much Too Young, Aladdin* (London Bubble).

Television credits include: *Doctors, EastEnders, Tough Love, Nature Boy, The Bill, The Locksmith, Body Story, Come Outside, Holby City* and most recently the *Anti Smoking* commercial for the British Heart Foundation.

Film credits include: *Raffle Baby, Plato's Breaking Point*. Radio credits include: *Grandfather's Feet, This Bitter Sweet Earth, Redeeming History, Shades of Black, Top Story*.

Neil is delighted to be back at the Theatre Royal re-living his parent's history.

Victor Romero-Evans Ferdy

Victor has worked extensively on stage, screen and radio since the 1970s. He is a founding member of the Black Theatre Co-operative and has appeared in many of their productions, including *Welcome Home Jacko* – incidentally Philip Hedley's first production as artistic director here, and now Victor is in his last production here too! *Redemption Song* and *Sixty-Five with a Bullet*. More recent stage credits include Tiata Fahodzi's *Abyssinia* and the central role of 'Papacita' in Talawa's *One Love* at the Lyric Theatre, Hammersmith. He has also worked with the *Black Theatre Forum* and *The Posse*, of which he is a founder member. Victor's television credits include *Holby City, Judge John Deed* (BBC) and 'Patrick Trueman' in *Alistair McGowan's Big Impression* (BBC). He also played 'Bellamy' in three series of *No Problem*. Film credits include *Class of Miss MacMichael, Babylon, Burning an Illusion, The Book Liberator* and *Marked for Death*. He was last seen here at Theatre Royal in *Ragamuffin*.

Chris Tummings Lennie

Chris trained at The Anna Scher Theatre and made his professional debut in 1979, in Mustapha Matura's *Welcome Home Jacko* at The Factory, and then the show transferred to the Theatre Royal Stratford East in 1983.

Chris is also a founder member of the Black Theatre Co-operative and has appeared in a number of their productions, both in the UK and on tour, including New York and South Korea, representing Great Britain for The International Theatre Council. Chris's most recent stage credit is in the West End production of *Buddy*.

In the eighties, Chris starred in LWT's cult TV sitcom *No Problem* playing 'Toshiba', the motor-mouth disc-jockey. Other television credits include: *Desmond's* (Channel 4), *Get Up, Stand Up*, which Chris also co-wrote (Channel 4), *Holding On* (BBC), *The Bill* (ITV) and *Doctors* (BBC).

Chris has also had major roles in the feature films: *Runners, Burning An Illusion* and *Water* alongside Michael Caine & Billy Connolly. It was *Water*, which saw Chris appear on stage alongside Eric Clapton, George Harrison & Ringo Starr!

Yaa Sybil

Trained at the Arts Educational School, Yaa has appeared in many musical theatre productions including 'Sarafina' in *The Lion King* (Lyceum Theatre); Simon Callow's production of *Carmen Jones* (Old Vic) and *Fame* (Cambridge Theatre). Other theatre credits include 'Heavenly' in Jonzie D's *Aeroplane Man* (Queen Elizabeth Hall); 'Inscrutable Lady' in Kerry Michael's *Aladdin* and 'Carrie' in Paulette Randall's production of *Shoot to Win*, both at Stratford East. Yaa has also modelled for Coca-Cola/Schweppes, Levis, Ebony and Vogue magazines. In between all of this, she managed to find time to choreograph her first musical *Passports to the Promised Land*, appeared on MTV Base Lounge with the band *The Projects*, also on Revelation TV with the gospel group *Chosen*, and is currently writing her debut album!

Creative Team

Paul Sirett Writer

The Big Life is Paul's fifth production at Stratford East, his previous productions were *A Night in Tunisia*, *Worlds Apart* (Best Play, Pearson); *Crusade* and *Jamaica House*. Other work for stage includes: *Rat Pack Confidential* (Nottingham Playhouse, Bolton Octagon, West End – Best Production, City Life); *Skaville* (Bedlam Theatre, Cockpit Theatre – Best Comedy nominee, Time Out); *This Other Eden* (Gilded Balloon, DoC); *International Café* (Chamber Theatre); *Dracula* (Second Thought Theatre – co-written with Jonathan Rix). Paul's radio work includes: *Vissi d'Arte* (IRDP – Medallist Best Writer, Finalist Best Drama, New York International Radio Festival & Special Commendation, Prix d'Italia); *Bad Vibrations* (Finalist Best Drama, New York International Radio Festival); *Hellhound on My Trail* (BBC); *The Blood of Eva Bergen* (BBC); *Gunchester* (BBC series – co-written with Steve Thomas). With co-writer, Jonathan Rix, Paul has written television comedy sketches for Curtis and Ishmael, Steve Coogan and Arthur Smith. He was Literary Manager at Soho Theatre for seven years and is currently Dramaturg for the Royal Shakespeare Company. Paul is an Associate Writer of the Theatre Royal Stratford East.

Paul Joseph Music

Paul Joseph has been the lead singer with his band the roots reggae band The Nazarites for seven years. They are managed by Paul McGuigan and are currently recording their first album due for release in the summer 2004. Paul plays most string and percussion instruments. He has guested on records for bands such as Cornershop who he has also remixed for and he has worked with musicians from Primal Scream and Teenage Fanclub.
Paul attended the Theatre Royal Musical Theatre Workshop in 1999, and is under commission to the Theatre Royal as a composer on another musical theatre piece *Carnival in Notting Hill* along with Lisa Levi (*Book* / Lyrics) and Alex Thomas (Co-composer). Paul was also involved in the workshopping of the *Da Boyz*! which went on to be produced at the Theatre Royal in 2003.

Clint Dyer Director

Clint started out at Stratford East as an actor with the Youth Theatre at 15 and worked his way up the ranks on stage and off culminating in acting for Mike Leigh in *It's A Great Big Shame* and then starring in Barrie Keeffe's *Sus*. Clint has acted extensively on TV, film and in theatre over the last 20 years in such things as *EastEnders*, *Prime Suspect II*, Linda La Plante's *Commando*, *Inspector Lynley Mysteries*, *Lock Stock*, etc, and films like *Shopping*, *The Low Down*, *Everyone Loves Sunshine*, *Mr In-Between* and soon to be seen starring in *Cherps*. Currently Clint is filming *Sahara*.
Clint's directing work was born out of the Theatre Royal's Directors Course. He was also part of the original Musical Theatre Workshop Committee and attended the Tisch School in New York to help build the Musical Theatre Workshop that has been going for five years at Theatre Royal Stratford East.

Jenny Tiramani Designer

Master of Clothing, Properties and Hangings – Jenny is Director of Theatre Design at Shakespeare's Globe, where her work includes designs for *Cymbeline*, *Hamlet*, *Twelfth Night* and *Richard II*. Jenny received the 2002 Laurence Olivier Award for Best Costume Design for *Twelfth Night*. Other close associations have been with the Theatre Royal Stratford East, designing for many new plays including the musical *Baiju Bawra* directed by ULTZ; Kenneth Branagh's Renaissance Theatre Company including *Hamlet* and *King Lear*; Mark Rylance and Claire van Kampen with whom she created *The Tempest*. She has also designed *Macbeth* (Phoebus Cart Company); *As You Like It* (Theatre for a New Audience, New York) and for 7:84 Theatre *Co.s* (England and Scotland) with John McGrath and Elizabeth MacLennan. Work in the West End includes *Steaming* (Comedy Theatre); *Much Ado About Nothing*, directed by Judi Dench (Phoenix); *Travelling Tales* with John Sessions (Haymarket); *Unforgettable* with Clark Peters (Garrick).

Robert Hyman Musical Director for Production

Robert returns to the Theatre Royal having previously written the music & lyrics for the millennium pantomime *Dick Whittington*, *20,000 Leagues Under the Sea* and this year's critically acclaimed *Red Riding Hood* as well as working as MD on *Cinderella*, *Aladdin*, *Make Some Noise* and *Jack and the Beanstalk*.
As a conductor he has worked all over the world, from the Sibelius Academy in Finland to Disneyland Paris, as well as BBC Radio and Television.
As a composer, he has written thirty scores. *A Tale of Two Cities* premiered at the Hackney Empire and reached the final of the Vivian Ellis Awards. *Hackback* (published by IMP) has played as far afield as Switzerland, South Africa and New Zealand. His musical versions of *The Happy Prince* and *A Little Princess* are currently touring the country with Image Theatre Company. As Musical Director his credits include: *Into the Woods*, *A Chorus Line*, *Snoopy!*, *Godspell*, *Sweet Charity* and variety shows at the London Palladium, The Dominion Theatre and the Theatre Royal Drury Lane.

Delroy Murray Musical Director for Performance

Delroy Murray has an extensive musical background, starting his own record label at seventeen, achieving several hit records both on his own label and with bands signed to London and EMI Records.
An adept all-round musician, Delroy's career has encompassed many types of music. He is currently a Director of The Song Corporation, a music publishing house. He also has a wealth of teaching experience and works as a mentor for the Borough of Waltham Forest, teaching song writing to young adults.
In 2001 Delroy, along with Hope Massiah, wrote his first musical for the Theatre Royal Stratford East, *One Dance Will Do*, a production which subsequently toured the East End. Hope and Delroy went on to write the words and music for Stratford East's pantomime *Jack and The Beanstalk*, and are now commissioned to write a new pantomime and an original musical.
Other credits include: composing the music for *The Real McCoy*, *Black Music Awards* (LWT), *Nights Out at The Empire* (Channel Four) and the *291 Club*.

Delroy is currently composing music for the new BBC2 series of *Baby Father*. The Delroy Murray Band has been backing various well known artists through Lover's Rock, R & B and Reggae.

Gerry Jenkinson Lighting Designer

Gerry started lighting bands in 1966. Since then has been lighting Citizens productions in Glasgow and internationally.

He has worked on numerous drama productions nationwide including: The National Theatre, The Royal Shakespeare Company, Old Vic, Royal Court, Hampstead, Almeida, Kings Head, Donmar, Stratford East, Richmond and Bush Theatre's.

Gerry has also worked abroad in: New York, Paris, Ludwigshafen, Dublin's Abbey and Gaiety.

Opera and Ballet for Covent Garden, English National, Scottish, Welsh, North, Kent, Glyndebourne, Aldeburgh, Buxton and Sadlers Wells.

Numerous West End credits include: *Rocky Horror Show*, *Gloo Joo*, *Mother Courage*, *The Vortex*, *Design for Living*, *Heat of the Day*, *Torch Song Trilogy*, *The Mystery of the Roe Bouquet*, *A Madhouse in Goa*, *The Entertainer*, *The Original Phantom of the Opera*, *The Invisible Man*, *Lady Windermere's Fan*, *A Woman of No Importance*, *Travels with my Aunt*, *Oleanna*, *Rupert Street Lonely Hearts Club*, *Giovanni D'Arco*, *The Pearl Fishers*, *Semi-Monde*.

Recently Gerry has been working on: *Golden Boy*, *Two Sisters and a Piano*, *True West*, *Barber of Seville*.

Production Credits

Casting Director	Dawn Reid
Costume Supervisor	Jo Poole
Assistant Stage Manager	Denise Furey
Scenic Construction	Capital Scenery Limited
Prop Maker	Ben Thomas
Costume Makers (Ladies)	Elsa Threadgold, Judith Ward
Tailors	Mr Bruno, Mr Edwards (Aeon Hands Tailoring)
Wardrobe Assistants	Maria Ditchencko, Mia Sanchez

Theatre Royal Stratford East Staff

Artistic

Artistic Director	Philip Hedley
Deputy Artistic Director	Kerry Michael
Resident Director	Dawn Reid
Associate Producer	Robert Miles
New Writing Manager	Ashmeed Sohoye
Writer In Residence	Hope Massiah
Senior Script Associate	Myra Brenner
Theatre Archivist	Murray Melvin
Assistant Archivist	Mary Ling

Musical Theatre Project

Associate Director	ULTZ
Associate Artists	Fred Carl, Clint Dyer, Suzanne Gorman, Robert Lee, Paulette Randall, Deborah Sathe, Zoe Simpson

Administration

Administrative Director	Belinda Kidd
Administrative Manager	Karen Fisher
Development Officer	Zareen Graves
Finance Manager	Paul Canova
Finance Assistant	Elinor Jones

Education

Head of Education	Caroline Barth
Youth and Education Officer	Karlos Coleman, Emma Finlayson

Marketing And Press

Head of Marketing and Sales	Barry Burke
Marketing Officer	Fiona Francis
Press Officer	Jasmine Cullingford
Young Persons	
Audience Development	Ayesha Harvey
Box Office Manager	Beryl Warner
Deputy Manager	Nicole Seraphin
Box Office Assistants	Asha Bhatti, Saif Osmani, Alice Cook, Davina Campbell, Sharlene Fulgence

Contacting the Theatre

Theatre Royal Stratford East
Gerry Raffles Square
Stratford
London
E15 1BN

Box Office   020 8534 0310
Administration   020 8534 7374
Fax   020 8534 8381
Minicom   020 8279 1114
Press Direct Line   020 8279 1123
Education Direct Line   020 8279 1107

e-mail   theatreroyal@stratfordeast.com
Website   www.stratfordeast.com

Offices open   Mon – Fri   10am-6pm
Box Office open   Mon – Sat   10am-7pm

Bar open   Mon – Sat   11am-11pm
Food served   Mon – Fri   12am – 2.30pm & 5pm – 7.30pm

Caribbean FLAVOURS

Caribbean Flavours in the Theatre Royal Bar

The finest fish and chicken spiced and cooked to perfection by our chef, Wills, as well as a wide range of non-Caribbean food, salads and snacks. Now available in the Theatre Royal Bar.

We would like to thank the Funders and Supporters of Theatre Royal Stratford East: Bridge House Trust, Calouste Gulbenkian Foundation, Esmée Fairbairn, Financial Services Authority, UBS, Ken Hill Trust, Paul Hamlyn Foundation, The Pidem Fund and Unity Theatre Trust.

We would like to thank: Guildhall School of Music and Drama and the Bush Theatre

Washing Powder supplied by Ecover.

Theatre Royal Stratford East would like to give special thanks to the Esmée Fairbairn Foundation.

THE BIG LIFE
The Ska Musical

Book and lyrics by Paul Sirett
Music by Paul Joseph

First published in 2004 by Oberon Books Ltd.
(incorporating Absolute Classics.)
521 Caledonian Road, London N7 9RH
Tel: 020 7607 3637/Fax: 020 7607 3629

e-mail: oberon.books@btinternet.com
www.oberonbooks.com

A catalogue record for this book is available from the British
Library.

ISBN: 1 84002 441 0

Cover design: ochee

Printed in Great Britain by Antony Rowe Ltd, Chippenham.

Characters

THE MEN	THE WOMEN
FERDY	ZULIEKA
BERNIE	SYBIL
LENNIE	MARY
DENNIS	KATHY
REVEREND	JACQUELINE
ADMIRAL/EROS	MRS APHRODITE

Other parts played by members of the cast and band.

Mrs Aphrodite is a member of the audience. She offers opinions and thoughts between scenes. At the time of going to print Mrs Aphrodite's interjections were not finalised.

For Natalie, Joe and Elena

'War over, and Big City begin to work on ship and travel all about. One day the ship dock in London and he went to Piccadilly Circus and watch the big life. When the ship sail Big City stay behind.'

Sam Selvon *The Lonely Londoners 1956*

Note
The following script was correct at the end of first week's rehearsals but may differ slightly from the play as performed.

ACT ONE

Scene 1

At finish of Overture lights dim. Curtain opens to reveal...

OPENING INSTRUMENTAL – Is It Love

...sea mist. As the mist clears we see the deck of a large ship somewhere at sea. The deck is deserted. ADMIRAL enters with his guitar. He looks out at the audience; he does a double-take... Music cue.

In Inglan

ADMIRAL: **Inglan...**

FERDY, LENNIE, DENNIS, BERNIE and SYBIL enter...

FERDY/LENNIE/DENNIS/SYBIL/BERNIE: **Inglan...**

Deck fills with passengers – REVEREND, CONNIE, ENA, JOYCE – all straining to get their first glimpse of England...

ALL: **Inglan...**
Big time – We comin
Inglan – We comin

Big time
In Inglan
Inglan

We comin
Motherland – We comin
Inglan – We comin

Big time – We comin...

Music continues – underscoring. A STEWARDESS enters. The REVEREND pushes through the crowd.

REVEREND: Let us pray!

The passengers sink to their knees in silent prayer.

(*After a moment – rising.*) Okay.

DENNIS: 'Okay'? What happen to 'Amen'?

LENNIE: Hey, I hear in Inglan they have snow.

DENNIS: It's becos it's cold, ennit.

29

LENNIE: I hear they have White Christmas.

DENNIS: Well, of course, man – White people: White Christmas.

ENA sneezes.

LENNIE: Bless yu.

CONNIE: (*To ENA.*) You know something, you need a hat. That is why you are sneezin, cos in Inglan everybody wear a hat. You neva know dat?

ENA: Me have a coat; don't have no hat.

CONNIE: You no have no hat! You finished now, you know.

FERDY: (*To BERNIE and SYBIL.*) So what kind of work you look for?

BERNIE: Engineering.

SYBIL: Office work for me, secretarial. But first, we get married.

JOYCE: You two gettin betroad! Congratulations!

SYBIL: Been together six year.

BERNIE: (*To FERDY.*) And you? What you do?

FERDY: I hope to be taking up a position in a university.

(*To LENNIE.*) You?

LENNIE: Get me some work in a garage, man. I can fix ennitin. Big car, small car – I the man! Cap-i-tan!

FERDY: (*To DENNIS.*) And what about you?

DENNIS: Ennitin man, long as me get plenty money.

FERDY: Do you have a trade?

DENNIS: Don't need one. I got dis!

Takes out a medal.

My brudder in the RAF. He get killed in de war. Shoot down over de Inglish Channel. Wid dis – I can do ennitin.

FERDY: Anything?

DENNIS: Ennitin.

LENNIE: Ennitin – such as?

DENNIS: Listen...

(*Sings.*) **Watchman – Stockman**

Craftsman – Draftsman
Mi dig a hole – Fish a shoal
Wash a bowl – Stick a sole
Shovel coal – Climb a pole
Mi getting an di payroll
Climin down di manhole
Forgettin all dat rigmarole
Mi neva lose mi self-control
Mi goana hav de las laff
Climin down de mineshaff
No mixin wid de riff-raff
Splittin nuttin haff an haff

BERNIE: I build a bridge
A big monument
Get me a commission
From the government

SYBIL: I type very fast
Sixty words a minnit
I have certificate
First prize, I win it
(*Spoken.*) Tell you…

ALL: Kyan wait to get to Inglan
Wi mek it big in a Inglan
Mek it rich and be a hot boy
Mek it all di way…
In a Inglan

BERNIE: (*To FERDY.*) So what you teach?

FERDY: Philosophy.

REVEREND: Really? What kind of thing?

FERDY: (*Spoken.*) Well let me see, there's

(*Sings.*) Kant and Hegel
Locke and Schlegel
There's politics and ethics
Catholic aesthetics
Mavericks
Like Liebnitz

I'll teach epistemology

31

Philosophy, philology
Phonology, ontology
And then phenomenology
And then there is Confucianism
Idealism, dualism
Talk about religious schism
And of course materialism

(*Spoken.*) I'm writing a book about the Stoics at the moment.
And you?

REVEREND: **I'll find me a church**
Steeple with a clock
A large vicarage
And preach to my flock

(*Spoken.*) Hallelujah!

ALL: **Kyan wait to get to Inglan**
Wi mek it big in a Inglan
Mek it rich an be a hot boy
Mek it all di way...
Kyan wait to get to Inglan
Wi mek it big in a Inglan
Mek it rich an be a hot boy
Mek it all di way...
In a Inglan

DENNIS: (*To LENNIE.*) You say you is a mechanic?

LENNIE: It go like dis...

(*Sings.*) **Big car – Small car**
Rolls Royce – Jaguar
Don't need no plan
Just give quick scan
With oil can
Spot broke piston
Cos I de man
Cap-i-tan
Me doin up de old crock
What you want is in stock
If you like I fix lock
An I work around de clock
Me give de car a good clean
New wiper on windscreen

Make it look a new machine
From old banger to limousine

(*To ADMIRAL.*) You?

ADMIRAL: **I play my song**
Hang out on de street
Gonna bring some lovin
To all dem dat I meet

(*Spoken.*) You know what I mean...

ALL: **Kyan wait to get to Inglan**
Wi mek it big in a Inglan
Mek it rich an be a hot boy
Mek it all di way...
Kyan wait to get to Inglan
Wi mek it big in a Inglan
Mek it rich an be a hot boy
Mek it all di way...
In a Inglan

BERNIE: **Engineer**
DENNIS: **Draper**
SYBIL: **Secretary**
DENNIS: **Baker**
FERDY: **Academic**
REVEREND: **Bishopric**
LENNIE: **Mechanic**
DENNIS: **Feeling sick**
SYBIL: **Get a bag**
BERNIE: **Double quick**

ALL: **Kyan wait to get to Inglan**
Wi mek it big in a Inglan
Mek it rich an be a hot boy
Mek it all di way...
Kyan wait to get to Inglan
Wi mek it big in a Inglan
Mek it rich an be a hot boy
Mek it all di way...
In a Inglan

ADMIRAL: The Big Life!

ALL: We comin!

Song finishes.

LENNIE produces a bottle of rum.

LENNIE: Rum!

FERDY: (*Declining the offer of a drink.*) Not for me, thank you. I tell you; I am determined to make something of myself. Nothing is going to stop me!

BERNIE: I'm with you!

LENNIE: Yeh, man. That go for me too!

DENNIS: An me!

FERDY: The sky is the limit!

LENNIE: That right!

BERNIE: There is no limit!

DENNIS: No, man!

FERDY: It's good to know there are others of a like-mind.

LENNIE: You bet you!

FERDY: Maybe we should get together?

BERNIE: Yeh! Hey, you have a place to stay?

LENNIE: No.

DENNIS: Me needer.

FERDY: I'm going to look when I get there.

BERNIE: Me and Sybil, my fiancée, we have the address of a B&B. (*Takes out piece of paper.*) 236 Boleyn Road, London, E7. Her sister stayin there. Maybe we can fix you boys up?

LENNIE: Sound good to me!

DENNIS: Yeh, man!

FERDY: Why not! Thank you...er...?

BERNIE: Bernie.

FERDY: The name is Ferdinand.

LENNIE: Lennie.

DENNIS: Dennis.

LENNIE: Hey, I propose a toast: To Inglan!

FERDY/BERNIE/DENNIS/LENNIE: Inglan!

ADMIRAL crosses to them.

ADMIRAL: (*Eyeing-up CONNIE and ENA.*) Hey, you boys see what I see?

LENNIE: I see! I see!

ADMIRAL: Them girls is hot hot hot hot hot hot.

BERNIE: I am suppose to be getting wed.

FERDY: I thought we was meant to be going to England to make something of ourselves – not chase woman.

LENNIE: We not there yet!

(*To DENNIS.*) Come...

LENNIE leads DENNIS to one side. During the opening section of the song SYBIL talks to a STRANGER. The conversation ends with the STRANGER giving SYBIL a hug. BERNIE sees this. When the STRANGER exits, SYBIL and BERNIE start to argue.

WE CAN

LENNIE: Listen close...

(*Sings conspiratorially.*) **Dem girl over dare
With dem ribbon in dem hair
Dem girl just a waitin for a man**

DENNIS: You think so?

LENNIE: **An if we take we chance
Like Douglas Fairbanks
We can hook dem if we do**

DENNIS: **You think we can?**
LENNIE: **I say we can**
DENNIS: **We can?**
LENNIE: **I know we can**
DENNIS: **We can**
LENNIE: **We can**
DENNIS: **We can**
LENNIE: **We can**
DENNIS: **We can**

CONNIE turns to look at LENNIE and DENNIS. LENNIE waves; CONNIE turns away without acknowledging him.

LENNIE: **We show dem how we buosi**
Talk bout de sonshain and make cosy
Me say dem girl just waitin for a man
An if we smile an sweet op
Jokify an rub op
We can hook dem if we do
I know we can

DENNIS: **You think we can?**
LENNIE: **Oh yes, we can**
DENNIS: **You sure we can?**
LENNIE: **We can**
We can
We can

LENNIE and DENNIS move in on CONNIE and ENA.

LENNIE: Me see you makin de most a de sonshain.

CONNIE and ENA ignore him. DENNIS tries to make an impression by throwing his jacket casually over his shoulder. The women aren't impressed.

DENNIS: (*To ENA.*) You a wear pretty dress.

LENNIE puts an arm around CONNIE.

CONNIE: (*Removing LENNIE's arm.*) I don't tink so.

LENNIE: Just a lickle fun me a make.

DENNIS puts on an enormous smile.

ENA: What you smilin at?

LENNIE: (*To CONNIE.*) You wan beautiful wan, you know.

CONNIE: An you are beginnin to rile me.

LENNIE: Don't get vex. We have a good time.

LENNIE laughs, he does a few nifty dance steps. DENNIS joins in. He mooches up to ENA.

DENNIS: Come ya, baby.

DENNIS rubs up against ENA. She pushes him away and he falls over at FERDY'S feet. CONNIE and ENA exit. FERDY and LENNIE help DENNIS to his feet.

FERDY: You all right?

DENNIS: (*Finds a tear in his trousers.*) Me trousa! Me trousa tier op!

LENNIE: Why dem girl vex so?

DENNIS: Me trousa!

LENNIE: Dem nuttin but a baks-about!

DENNIS: Me best trousa!

LENNIE: **Dem mussa tink we fool**
Dem no tink we go a school

DENNIS: **Me try to nice her op**
But she go get all hetop

LENNIE: **I tell you**
I tell you
I tell you
I tell you – dem girls is too much badarieshan

LENNIE/DENNIS: **Girls!**

The argument between BERNIE and SYBIL has reached boiling point.

SYBIL: That's it! Finished!

SYBIL storms off.

BERNIE: Sybil! Sybil!

LENNIE: (*To BERNIE.*) **Give it op!**
Give it op!
Give it op!
Give it op! – Dem girls is too much badarieshan

LENNIE/DENNIS: **Girls!**

LENNIE: Why we badda?

FERDY: I was just asking myself the same question.

DENNIS: Too much badarieshan.

LENNIE: They always have to get their way.

LENNIE: **Manipulate us**
FERDY: **Denegrate us**
DENNIS: **Separate us**
LENNIE: **Aggravate us**
DENNIS: **Everytin just how dem say.**

LENNIE: **Dem tell you wen to get up**
Dem tell you wen to sit

DENNIS: **Dem tell go an do dat**
Den com here an do dis

LENNIE: **Dem tell you 'I got hedache'**
Or 'I got de bellywurk'
Dem take you for a dumb ass

DENNIS: **Take you for a jerk**

LENNIE: **Dem ful a 'com here darlin'**
Wen dem get it in dem head

DENNIS: **Dem ful a 'com here big boy'**
Wen dem want you build a shed

LENNIE: **Dem say 'go fix de baart tob'**
'Go mend de fence an gayt'
'Go paint de door an skirtin'
'Go repayr an restaarait'

DENNIS: **Dem say 'you got no mannaz'**
'You eat jus like a daag'
'You snaa jus like a dangkee'
'You smell jus like a haag'
'Yu luk jus like a cod fish'
'Yu shud bi in a zoo'

LENNIE: **But wen dem want a freegidair**
Dem full of

DENNIS/LENNIE: **'I love you'**

Song finishes.

ADMIRAL: Ah, you boys, you know, you make me laff. I tell you: you don't know how to talk to woman. I show you...

IS IT LOVE

(Sings to CONNIE and ENA.) **When I look into your eyes**
I see paradise
When you put your hand in mine
I can feel the sunshine
When we walk upon the sand
I think I understand
When we kiss beneath the coconut tree
I want to sing...

ADMIRAL dances with CONNIE and ENA.

ADMIRAL/CONNIE/ENA:
> **Is it love love love**
> **Is it love love love**
> **Is it love love love**
> **That I am feeling**
> **Oh-oh-oh**

> **Is it love love love**
> **Is it love love love**
> **Is it love love love**
> **That I am feeling**
> **Oh-oh-oh**

As ADMIRAL finishes his song the REVEREND stands on a bench and begins an impromptu sermon.

REVEREND: Brothers and Sisters, we must resist the sins of the flesh. Allow not the sin of lust to lead us into temptation. Only in purity can man succeed. Purity of mind. And purity of flesh. Loose morals lead us to Hell. Hell! This is what the Bible tells us.

Points to FERDY, LENNIE and DENNIS.

You are in very great danger. You sin every time you look upon a woman with lust. A punishment greater than any pain man can imagine awaits you. Sinners! Repent before it is too late. Take refuge from the heaving, sweaty, steaming jungle of human flesh. Resist the devil. Resist temptation...

The REVEREND exits. SYBIL passes in front of BERNIE.

BERNIE: Sybil!

SYBIL: Don't talk to me!

SYBIL exits. BERNIE looks devastated. FERDY, LENNIE and DENNIS cross to him.

LENNIE: What she do?

BENNIE: That's it. Just like that. Six years we were together.

FERDY: Typical.

BERNIE: We were suppose to be getting married.

LENNIE: So wh'appen?

BERNIE: Another man.

39

FERDY: (*Hands BERNIE his handkerchief.*) Here…

LENNIE: You betta off widout her.

BERNIE: No.

FERDY: Women are the root of all our problems.

DENNIS: Yeh.

BERNIE: Six years.

FERDY: Six wasted years. Just imagine what you could've achieved in that time. Pull yourself together. You're not the first. Tell you – never trust a woman.

Music cue.

BERNIE: What do you know!

FERDY: Sit down.

BERNIE: Leave me alone.

FERDY: Sit down and listen!

FERDY pushes BERNIE down onto a bench.

Never Trust a Woman

FERDY: A word of advice…

(*Sings.*) **Never never never never**
Never never never never
Never never trust a woman

BERNIE: You don't know what you're talking about.

FERDY: Is that so? Let me tell you a story…

(*Sings.*) **I was researching my PhD**
At West Indies University
When I met this woman you see

LENNIE: I see.

FERDY: **She was tall and slim and intelligent**
And twenty years older than me

DENNIS: Twenty yeaz!

LENNIE: Old enuff fi be you granny!

BERNIE: What happened?

FERDY: **For a year I worship, I adore**
There'll never be another, I swore

LENNIE: Yeh yeh…

FERDY: **Then one day my jaw bone hit the floor**
When I find out she's the wife
Of a judge from Ecuador

BERNIE: What!

FERDY: She tell her husband about us.

LENNIE: No!

FERDY: And he knows the vice chancellor of my University. Has me thrown out. My heart broken. My career over. And it's all because of her. But I got over it. I put her out of my mind.

BERNIE: What did she say?

FERDY: She said… It was fun while it lasted.

BERNIE: And that was it?

FERDY: (*Tearful.*) Yes.

LENNIE: Crewel.

DENNIS: Crewel.

FERDY: And that is why I say…

FERDY/LENNIE/DENNIS: **Never never never never**
Never never never never
Never never trust a woman

BERNIE goes to stand up.

LENNIE: Sit down…

(*Sings.*) **I was fixin dis ole push-foot down town**
Wen de daata a de house come round
Well, you know me like to ack de clown
So me joke an me fool and me funny ha-ha-ha
But her Faada catch me wid me trousa down

DENNIS: No!

BERNIE: What did you say?

LENNIE: Nuttin. I run.

FERDY: Coward.

LENNIE: Her Faada a him a de baddis man ina de distrik!

BERNIE: So what happen?

41

LENNIE: **Three mont later me waitin at de alta**

BERNIE: No!

LENNIE: **Her Faada walta say you will exaalt her**
  Me try to say to him, it is not my fault, sir
  Im say, Lennie you will com live with me
  Mi tink, me emigrate to Malta

FERDY: You married her?

LENNIE: What else could I do!

BERNIE: So what you doing here?

LENNIE: **A few week later she say she sick a me**
  All me drinkin, gamblin, womanisin see
  I say, I sick a you, always act like you queen bee
  Me drink two quaat a rum set fire to de goat
  She want a D-I-V-O-R-C-E

  (*Spoken.*) Then, two days ago her Fadda come look fi me, wavin im bill-hook. Me see her standin at de gayt, laafin at me.

BERNIE: What you do?

LENNIE: I run!

DENNIS: Crewel

LENNIE: Me tell you...

FERDY/LENNIE/DENNIS: **Never never never never**
  Never never never never
  Never never trust a woman

BERNIE: What about you?

LENNIE: Im never had a girl.

DENNIS: Me have!

LENNIE: Who?

DENNIS: Tryphena.

LENNIE: Figment of im imaginashan.

DENNIS: We engayge. (*Pulls out a photo – shows it to BERNIE.*) She a beautiful wan.

BERNIE: What she do?

DENNIS: Hairdresser.

LENNIE: You tell me she a nurse.

DENNIS: She got a new job.

FERDY: And I suppose you think she's back home waiting for you? Huh? At this very moment she could be anywhere. With anyone.

DENNIS: No.

FERDY: Doing anything.

DENNIS: No!

FERDY/LENNIE/BERNIE: **Never never never never
Never never never never
Never never trust a woman**

Segue into next song.

FERDY: I have a suggestion.

ADMIRAL eavesdrops.

BERNIE: I hope it's a good one.

THE CONTRACT SONG

FERDY: **If we are serious
The time has come to act
If we want betterment
Then we should make a pact
An agreement to work hard
Save all the money that we earn
To study and to be someone
Fore time come to return**

LENNIE: Sound like a good idea to me.

DENNIS: Yeh, man!

FERDY: I'll draw something up.

Taking notebook and pencil from his pocket – sings as he writes.

**Item one
A day a week to fast**

BERNIE: What?

FERDY: **To make our money last
Item two
No alcohol, no cigarette
An indulgence we must forget**

Item three
We sleep four hours in a night
Make time to study, work and write
Item four
No relation with woman

BERNIE/LENNIE/DENNIS: What!

FERDY: **On this there must be a ban**

LENNIE: No relation with woman?

FERDY: That is what I said.

> (*Sings.*) **Now we must sign our names**
> **And discount all our fears**
> **By this we will be bound**
> **For a period of three years**

LENNIE: Three yeaz!

BERNIE: Impossible.

FERDY: Not if we do it properly.

BERNIE: We'll never stick to it.

FERDY: We can do anything we put our minds to.

> (*Sings.*) **Just think what you could have**
> **With no woman in your life**
> **All the money you could save**
> **No aggravation from no wife**
> **And when you get back home**
> **You will be a wealthy man**
> **Be the envy of your friend**
> **Have all the woman that you can**
> **And all them doubting people**
> **With them stuck up airs and graces**
> **Said you'd mount to nothing**

> (*Spoken.*) You know the kind of people I mean…

> (*Sings.*) **Picture the look pon their faces**

LENNIE: S'pose it only three yeaz.

DENNIS: Me can do dat.

FERDY: It's easy. Just remind yourself…

> (*Sings.*) **Item one**

LENNIE/DENNIS: **A day a week to fast**

FERDY: What for?

LENNIE/DENNIS: **To make our money last**

FERDY: **Item two**
LENNIE/DENNIS: **No alcohol, no cigarette**
FERDY: **An indulgence we must forget**

   Item three
LENNIE/DENNIS: **We sleep four hours in a night**

FERDY: Why?

LENNIE/DENNIS: **Make time to study, work and write**

FERDY: **Item four**
LENNIE/DENNIS: **No relation with woman**
FERDY: **On this there must be a ban**

BERNIE: Wait, wait. I agree we need to make the most of ourselves but we would be putting ourselves in a very difficult situation.

FERDY: Why do you have to keep finding fault?

BERNIE: Because it won't work.

FERDY: Good. Fine. Go and find Sybil.

BERNIE: No, listen… Let me read it properly.

FERDY hands the book to BERNIE.

FERDY: I may be willing to accept some minor amendments.

BERNIE: (*Sings.*) **Item one**
FERDY/LENNIE/DENNIS: **A day a week to fast**
BERNIE: **To make our money last**

FERDY: **Item two**
BERNIE: **No alcohol, no cigarette**
FERDY/LENNIE/DENNIS: **An indulgence we must forget**

BERNIE: **Item three**
FERDY/LENNIE/DENNIS: **We sleep four hours in a night**
BERNIE: **Make time to study, work and write**

FERDY: **Item four**
BERNIE: **No relation with woman**
BERNIE/FERDY/LENNIE/DENNIS: **On this there must be a ban**

ADMIRAL steps in – stops the band playing.

ADMIRAL: Hold on! Hold on! Wait, wait, wait... So what you do if you see a beautiful woman?

FERDY: We will train ourselves to deny our base instincts.

ADMIRAL: Man, you is ga-ga.

FERDY: I don't think so.

ADMIRAL: Mad as a hatta!

FERDY: We'll see about that.

ADMIRAL: I bet you five pound you will fail. Each an every one of you.

FERDY: (*Shaking ADMIRAL's hand.*) And we accept your bet.

BERNIE: We do?

ADMIRAL: Shake!

ADMIRAL grabs BERNIE's hand and shakes it. He shakes hands with LENNIE and DENNIS. FERDY finishes scribbling in his notebook.

FERDY: (*To BERNIE.*) Sign...

BERNIE hesitates.

ADMIRAL: I win.

BERNIE: Ah, what the hell!

BERNIE signs.

This is insane.

(*Handing the notebook and pencil to LENNIE.*) I'll tell you something, I might be the only man to speak out, but I bet I'll be the last one to give in.

LENNIE: (*Signs.*) We see about dat.

DENNIS: (*Signs.*) Yeh – Jus wait an see.

FERDY: (*Signs.*) There! All done! Believe me, the next three years will fly by.

ADMIRAL: (*Sings a melancholy reprise of the chorus from IS IT LOVE.*)
Is it love love love
Is it love love love
Is it love love love

That I am feeling...

Fog horn. The ship enters the harbour. The deck fills with passengers carrying their luggage.

FERDY: Well, this is it...

Music cue.

IN INGLAN (Reprise.)

ALL: **Inglan – We comin**
Big time – We comin
Kyan wait to get to Inglan
Wi mek it big in a Inglan
Mek it rich an be a hot boy
Mek it all di way...
Kyan wait to get to Inglan
Wi mek it big in a Inglan
Mek it rich an be a hot boy
Mek it all di way...
In a Inglan

They disembark.

ADMIRAL: The Big Life!

LENNIE: Brrrrrrr... It's cold!

Blackout.

Scene 2

Interior: Boarding house kitchen.

ZULIEKA, MARY and KATHY listening to the weather forecast on the wireless.

WEATHERMAN: ...freezing fog, hail and sleet across the country. And that's the outlook for this weekend.

MARY switches off the wireless. The doorbell rings; she shrieks and runs out. She re-enters a moment later with a dejected SYBIL, suitcases, et cetera.

MARY: Zulieka, Kathy – my step-sister, Sybil. Sybil, darlin!

MARY gives SYBIL a huge hug.

ZULIEKA: Pleased to meet you.

KATHY: Mary has told us a great deal about you.

ZULIEKA: Cup of char?

SYBIL: Yes, please.

MARY: So where is he? Where that man a yours?

SYBIL starts to cry.

What is it? Hey, what a matta?

Music cue.

SYBIL: We split up…

THAT MAN

MARY: But…You come here to get wed…I bet I know who behind this!
(*To ZULIEKA and KATHY.*) Sybil's father…

(*Sings.*) **He don't want them together
Said he would not permit it ever**

(*Spoken.*) What happen? What him a do?

SYBIL: Not him. Bernie…

(*Sings.*) **He saw me talking to another man
He gets so jealous, that's how it began**

(*Spoken.*) Vincent was on the boat.

MARY: Uncle Vincent!

SYBIL: Yes. I used to talk to him most mornings.

MARY: An this make Bernie jealous?

SYBIL: He don't know who Uncle Vincent is. He never met none a our family sept me an you an Avril, you know that. Uncle Vincent try and persuade me not to go through with it.

(*To ZULIEKA and KATHY.*) See my father don't want me to marry no Bajan. Thinks I should wed this rich Jamaican he's got line up. What I don't know is Bernie, he's been spying on me and Vincent. Every morning. Getting jealous. Then, today, he gets real sour. All this bile. And I get to thinking maybe my father is right, maybe Bernie isn't the one for me. We have this nasty, nasty row. And that's it. Over. I don't even know where he is.

(*Sings.*) **Now we'll never be together
But we promised ourselves forever**

I always thought he was the one
Now I'm alone, here in London

MARY: Why you not tell him who it is?

SYBIL: If he thought the family was tryin to interfere again – well, I don't know what him a do. Anyway, too late now.

SYBIL dissolves into tears.

MARY: Oh, Sybil, Sybil…

ZULIEKA: House rule number one: no crying over men.

KATHY: You can always get back together.

SYBIL shakes her head.

MARY: Im come back wid im tail between im leg. I see to dat!

SYBIL: (*Shakes her head.*) He's given up women.

ZULIEKA/MARY/KATHY: What!

SYBIL: For three years.

ZULIEKA/MARY/KATHY: What!

SYBIL: Him and three others. So they can better themselves.

ZULIEKA/MARY/KATHY: What!

SYBIL: Because women get in the way.

ZULIEKA/MARY/KATHY: Huh!

MARY: That man a fool!

KATHY: Lord have mercy.

ZULIEKA: You are better off without him.

MARY: **What the hell is wrong with**
ZULIEKA/MARY/KATHY: **That man**
KATHY: **What is going on with**
ZULIEKA/MARY/KATHY: **That man**
ZULIEKA: **Act like he is King Kong**
ZULIEKA/MARY/KATHY: **That man**

SYBIL: **What did I do**
  I did nothing wrong
  I did nothing bad to
  That man

MARY: Men aren't wort the trouble.

KATHY: Lord!

ZULIEKA: House rule number two: forget that man.

(*Sings.*) **Gotta get rid**
Betta rid of
ZULIEKA/MARY/KATHY: **That man**

MARY: **Just a big kid**
Betta rid of
ZULIEKA/MARY/KATHY: **That man**

SYBIL: **Nothing I did**
ZULIEKA/MARY/KATHY: **Betta rid of**
  That man

SYBIL: **Nothing I hid**
ZULIEKA/MARY/KATHY: **Betta rid of**
  That man

ALL: **Betta rid of – Get shot of – The lot of**
  Them men
  Betta rid of – Get shot of – The lot of
  Them men

Music continues – underscoring.

MARY: Women, parties an cars. All dem interest in.

ZULIEKA: Full of hot air. Boastful, bragging, swaggering. Best thing I ever did – get rid of my husband. Big fat, dribbling half-wit! Jump on you like you're an animal, do his thing, then fall fast asleep on top of you like a sack of potatoes.

KATHY: You ever use a toilet after one a dem?

MARY: Mmm hmm...

KATHY: It is a medical fact women are more intelligent than men.

ZULIEKA: Who starts wars?

SYBIL: Who comes up with stupid ideas to give up the opposite sex for three years!

WOMEN: **Betta rid of – Get shot of – The lot of**
  Them men
  Betta rid of – Get shot of – The lot of
  Them men

ZULIEKA: I'll fix your bed.

ZULIEKA exits.

MARY: I tell you, Sybil. What happen to you may be a blessin.

KATHY: Amen.

SYBIL: So how many live here?

MARY: Right now, just me and Kathy and Zulieka – it's her ex-husband's B&B. Two other girls and dis ole man just move out.

KATHY: It's hard to find somewhere. But I always say, the Lord will provide.

SYBIL: She seem nice – Zulieka.

MARY: Reckon she a Princess.

SYBIL: True?

MARY: Mmm hmm…

ZULIEKA re-enters.

ZULIEKA: I'll show you to your room.

KATHY: Here, let me take your bag.

MARY: I have a spare blanket I can borrow you.

ZULIEKA: And don't worry about that man.

WOMEN: (*Singing as they exit.*) **Betta rid of
Get shot of – The lot of
Them men**

Blackout.

Scene 3

Interior: Tube train.

ADMIRAL, FERDY, BERNIE, LENNIE and DENNIS exhausted, squashed together in a tube train, trying to read a map as the train hurtles between stations.

ADMIRAL: (*To audience.*) It not easy finding you way around a big city you never know.

FERDY: Reading map, attempting to pronounce unfamiliar place names. Chiz-wick Park… Turn-ham-Green…

ADMIRAL: (*To audience.*) Specially when you got nowhere to go.

LONDON SONG

LENNIE/DENNIS/BERNIE:
  Harrow, Hammersmith
  Highgate, Hampstead
  Wapping, Wimbledon,
  Wembley, Wanstead
  Shoreditch, Stamford Hill,
  Shadwell, Stratford
  Ongar, Osterley,
  Oval, Old Ford

FERDY:
  We do the right thing
  I hope and I pray
  Can't find no room
  Nowhere to stay

FERDY/LENNIE/DENNIS:
  Aldwych, Acton Town
  Angel, Aldgate
  Mile End, Marble Arch,
  Morden, Moorgate
  Barking, Bayswater,
  Brixton, Balham
  Fairlop, Farringdon,
  Finchley, Fulham

BERNIE:
  I don't want to be here
  Fed up in the smog
  Signs say: No Blacks
  No Irish and No Dogs

FERDY/BERNIE/DENNIS:
  There's Kentish Town
  And Camden Town
  And Canning Town
  Lord's Cricket Ground
  And Chorleywood
  And Hinchley Wood
  And Borehamwood
  And South Woodford

LENNIE:
  Miss home already
  Only here one day
  Don't understand thing
  Want to run away

BERNIE/LENNIE/FERDY:
  And Dollis Hill
  And Notting Hill
  And Muswell Hill
  And Rosherville
  And Golders Green
  And Parsons Green
  And Stepney Green
  And then East Sheen

DENNIS: We travel around
Say 'How do you do'
It's then I find out
I left my bag at Waterloo
(*Spoken.*)
I got nuttin to wear.

BERNIE/FERDY/DENNIS:
  And Forest Gate
  And New Cross Gate

LENNIE:
  Oh what we doing
  I want to go home

And Barnet Gate
And then Mortlake

DENNIS/BERNIE/LENNIE:
   And Shpherd's Bush
   And Latton Bush
   And Thresher's Bush
   And Enfield Wash

FERDY:
Hostels all full
Can't get a room

DENNIS/FERDY/BERNIE:
   And Manor Park
   And Tufnell Park
   And Upton Park
   And then there's Clerk-

BERNIE:
People don't want us
What did we do?

FERDY/BERNIE/LENNIE:
   -enwell
   Mill Hill
   And Notting Hill
   And Primrose Hill
   And Ladywell

DENNIS:
Got nothing to wear
Me clothes lost at
Waterloo

FERDY/LENNIE/
DENNIS/BERNIE:
   We been everywhere
   Can't find no place to stay
   No room anywhere
   They just send us away
   Just send us away
   Just send us away

ADMIRAL: Why don't you boys try that B&B Bernie tell you about?

BERNIE: No! Never! I would rather sleep on the street!

Tube train stops.

ADMIRAL: Ah well... My stop. Come see me when you change your mind about woman.

ADMIRAL steps off the train. The tube hurtles off into the distance.

ADMIRAL: (*Sings to self as he exits.*) **Is it love love love
Is it love love love...**

Lights down.

Scene 4

Interior: Boarding House Kitchen.

ZULIEKA, MARY, KATHY at breakfast. SYBIL enters.

MARY: Sleep okay?

SYBIL: Is it always that cold at night?

MARY: That wasn't cold, sis. Just you wait till it's really cold.

There is a knock at the front door.

ZULIEKA: Excuse me.

ZULIEKA exits.

MARY: So what your plan this morning?

SYBIL: Find work.

MARY: You could try dem Lyons Corner House. Them usually looking for casual staff.

SYBIL: I have qualifications.

ZULIEKA re-enters with BERNIE, LENNIE, DENNIS and FERDY.

Music cue.

ZULIEKA: (*Speaking as she enters.*) ...no swearing, no drinking, no fighting. One of you make trouble, all of you out. Do I make myself clear?

FERDY: I promise you'll have no trouble from us.

ZULIEKA: This way.

ZULIEKA exits.

DENNIS: (*Exiting.*) Lennie, could you borrow me a vest, man? Just till me suitcase turn up?

FERDY, LENNIE and DENNIS follow ZULIEKA off. BERNIE hangs behind.

BERNIE: There was no option. Believe me, this is the last place I want to be. Soon as I find another room, I'll be out.

MARY: You bet you will!

SYBIL: Mary. Don't.

BERNIE exits.

KATHY: Is that...?

MARY: Sybil, you okay?

KATHY: Is that him? Is that them?

SYBIL: Yes.

KATHY: Lord have mercy. And that was your...?

SYBIL: Bernie. Yes.

MARY: Huh! You hear him? 'This is the last place I want to be'!

SYBIL: How dare he come here!

MARY: That's men all over, never a thought for no one but themself!

THAT MAN (Reprise.)

MARY: Always have to be in the right.

(*Sings.*) **Be a sermonizer**
SYBIL/KATHY: **That man**

MARY: And you see the one with the glasses. Come all hoity-toity, think him better than everyone else.

(*Sings.*) **Be a patronizer**
SYBIL/KATHY: **That man**

MARY: And the stringy looking one in the trilby – think him God's gift?

(*Sings.*) **Be a womanizer**
SYBIL/KATHY: **That man**

KATHY: And the one in the Pork Pie hat?

MARY: **Smell like fertilizer**

SYBIL/KATHY: **That man**

SYBIL: **What did I do**
I did nothing wrong
I did nothing bad to
That man

MARY: Men! Tell you, they are the cause of all our problems. Turn the charm on and off like a lectric light switch.

SYBIL: Yes! When them want something!

KATHY: True.

MARY: Idle.

SYBIL: Good for nothing.

KATHY: Rude.

SYBIL: **What the hell is wrong with**

SYBIL/MARY/KATHY: **Them man**

SYBIL: **What the hell's going on with**
SYBIL/MARY/KATHY: **Them man**

SYBIL: **Act like they are King Kong**
SYBIL/MARY/KATHY: **Them men**
    Gotta get rid of – Get shot of – The lot of
    Them men
    Get rid of – Get shot of – The lot of
    Them men
    Them men
    No no, no no, no no
    Them men
    Oh no, no no, no no (*Et cetera.*)

SYBIL, MARY and KATHY exit singing.

Blackout.

Scene 5

Exterior: Piccadilly Circus.

Afternoon. ADMIRAL and JACQUELINE sitting together. ADMIRAL strumming the chords to EXCUSE ME. *JACQUELINE eating a bag of chips. MARY crosses the stage, arm in arm with her sister, SYBIL. LENNIE and DENNIS enter.*

DENNIS: Admiral!

ADMIRAL: You boys look fit to drop.

LENNIE: We look for work.

DENNIS: Nuttin.

LENNIE: We go all over. I tell them, back home I never have to look for work, work come look for me. I say, no car been made I can't fix. Tell dem, you got a problem, I the man! Cap-i-tan!

DENNIS: We say we do ennitin. But no one got any job.

LENNIE: We try bildin site.

DENNIS: Nuttin.

LENNIE: We try warehouse. We try factory.

DENNIS: Nuttin.

FERDY enters.

ADMIRAL: Hey, professor! I hope you have better luck than you friends here.

FERDY: What do you mean?

ADMIRAL: At your university.

FERDY: I'm just waiting for them to reply to a letter I sent. In the meantime I intend to find some translation work.

ADMIRAL: Good luck. So how you boys like it in Inglan?

DENNIS: It strange.

ADMIRAL: How you mean?

DENNIS: Man, all the trees is dead. And the sun...the sun is cold! How dat happen?

ADMIRAL: You find somewhere to stay?

LENNIE: Just tempree. You?

ADMIRAL: I stay with my friend for a while. (*Looks over at JACQUELINE.*) Want to say hello?

LENNIE: Come. We get a bus.

DENNIS: What about Bernie?

LENNIE: He can catch us.

DENNIS: We can walk.

LENNIE: Walk? Man, we walk fifty mile already today!

DENNIS: I don't like dem bus.

ADMIRAL: I hear there plenty work on dem buses.

LENNIE: Yeh? We go check it tomorrow.

DENNIS: Okay. But I don't wan catch no bus now.

ADMIRAL: What's wrong wid a bus?

DENNIS: Can't figure out how them thing work, man. This morning we catch a number 25 and some fella haul me off and give it:

'Excuse me, but I think you'll find I was in the queue before you.' I see a bus; I get on a bus. What the problem?

Music cue.

EXCUSE ME

DENNIS: Tell you, people here mighty peculiar.

(*Sings.*) **Them chew through the smog**
With them faces like a ghost

LENNIE: **Them stare when you pass**
Like some disease diagnosed

FERDY: **And all the time I'm thinking**
Just what did I do

DENNIS: **You get on a bus and it**

LENNIE/DENNIS/FERDY/ADMIRAL: (*Spoken – Upper Class British accent.*) 'Excuse me, but I think you'll find I was in the queue before you.'

LENNIE: And them clothes, man.

DENNIS: Yes, yes – them knitted face-mask ting with them eyes peering out.

FERDY: **They walk with them head down**
Steam coming out their mouth

DENNIS: **You try to say 'good maanin'**
Dem tink you are a lout

LENNIE: **And all the time I'm thinking**
Just what did I do

ADMIRAL: **You go to catch a film and it**

LENNIE/DENNIS/FERDY/ADMIRAL: (*Spoken – Upper Class British accent.*) 'Excuse me but I think you'll find I was in the queue before you.'

BERNIE enters.

ADMIRAL: Well, look now, if it isn't de engineer man. How you like the big city?

BERNIE: Great place to get a door slammed in your face!

(*Sings.*) **All the time I'm thinking**
Just what did I do

LENNIE: **You go to buy a stamp and it**

LENNIE/DENNIS/FERDY/ADMIRAL/BERNIE: (*Spoken –
Upper Class British accent.*) 'Excuse me, but I think you'll find I
was in the queue before you.'

DENNIS: **Tickety-boo**
ADMIRAL: **Sling your hook**
FERDY: **Up the apples and pears**
LENNIE: **Geezer**
BERNIE: **Guv'nor**
DENNIS: **Why can't them just say stairs**
FERDY: **La-di-da**
ADMIRAL: **Barnet Fair**
LENNIE: **Want to buy some snout?**
BERNIE: **On yer bike**
ADMIRAL: **Tellin porkies**

LENNIE/DENNIS/FERDY/ADMIRAL/BERNIE: **What them
on about?**

DENNIS: I'm hungry.

JACQUELINE: Chip?

DENNIS: Tank you.

LENNIE: I don't know how you can eat them chip, man. The food
here is nasty.

(*To ADMIRAL.*) You taste it?

ADMIRAL: Yeh, I taste it.

LENNIE: Well, you lucky, man, cos I damn sure I can't taste it.

(*Sings.*) **Fish and chip**
DENNIS: **Mushy pea**
BERNIE: **Cup of Oxo**
FERDY: **Not for me**
BERNIE: **Pie and mash**
ADMIRAL: **Jellied eel**
LENNIE: **Powdered egg**
BERNIE: **Don't appeal**

JACQUELINE: It's an acquired taste.

BERNIE: Well I hope I never acquire it.

LENNIE: It's no wonder they have rationing – too much of that food would kill you.

FERDY: **And all the time I'm thinking**
Just what did I do

BERNIE: **You go to buy a loaf and it**

LENNIE/DENNIS/FERDY/ADMIRAL/BERNIE: (*Spoken – Upper Class British accent.*) 'Excuse me, but I think you'll find I was in the queue before you.'

Song finishes.

REVEREND enters with his flock – including KATHY.

ADMIRAL: Hey, you boys want to buy some pepper sauce or some tinned breadfruit?

LENNIE: Where you get that?

DENNIS: Admiral, I don't suppose you have a spare pair of sock you could borrow me?

FERDY: (*Referring to the REVEREND.*) Isn't that…? Wasn't he on the boat?

ADMIRAL: Oh no! Come here sermonizing every day. Drive me crazy.

LENNIE: And look the frumpy one from the B&B.

REVEREND launches into his sermon from the steps of Eros. He addresses the sermon directly at ADMIRAL.

REVEREND: Beware the Circle of Woe!

ADMIRAL: Here we go…

REVEREND: Idleness begets sloth, sloth begets indolence, indolence begets intemperance, intemperance begets licentiousness, licentiousness begets idleness. Beware the Circle of Woe! A man must work! Beware the Circle of Woe! Let us pray.

They pray.

DENNIS: Please God let me get a job tomorrow; even if it mean Lennie don't get one.

LENNIE: What you say?

DENNIS: Man, I don't want no Circle of Woe!

ADMIRAL: (*To DENNIS – referring to the REVEREND.*) Take no notice of him.

REVEREND: Flee from idleness!

FLOCK: Flee!

ADMIRAL takes a swig from a bottle of rum.

REVEREND: Flee from the sins of the bottle!

FLOCK: Flee!

ADMIRAL puts an arm around JACQUELINE.

REVEREND: Flee from the sins of the flesh.

FLOCK: Flee!

ADMIRAL begins to busk Is It Love.

ADMIRAL: **When I look into your eyes
I see paradise**

REVEREND: Flee from the Devil's music!

FLOCK: Flee!

ADMIRAL: **When you put your hand in mine
I can feel the sunshine**

REVEREND attempts to counter ADMIRAL by singing ONWARD CHRISTIAN SOLDIERS.

REVEREND: **Onward Christian soldiers**

JACQUELINE joins in with ADMIRAL.

ADMIRAL: **When we walk upon the sand**

I think I understand

The REVEREND's flock joins in with him.

REVEREND/FLOCK: **Marching as to war**

ADMIRAL/JACQUELINE: (*Singing louder.*)
**When we kiss beneath the coconut tree
I want to sing…**

REVEREND/FLOCK: **With the cross of Jesus
Going on before** (*Et cetera.*)

ADMIRAL/JACQUELINE: **Is it love love love
Is it love love love** (*Et cetera.*)

REVEREND/FLOCK/ADMIRAL/JACQUELINE continue in their efforts to outdo each other.

LENNIE: (*To DENNIS.*) What you mean you don't want me to get a job?

DENNIS: Man, I don't mean it like dat!

LENNIE: Well how do you mean it!

BERNIE: Quiet down!

LENNIE: Don't you tell me 'quiet down'!

FERDY: Let's not argue.

LENNIE: I want to argue!

A huge row blows up between LENNIE, BERNIE, DENNIS, and FERDY. REVEREND/FLOCK and ADMIRAL and JACQUELINE get louder and louder. Bedlam. Eventually KATHY loses her temper.

KATHY: (*Very loud.*) Be Quiet!!!!!

Silence.

Blackout.

Scene 6

Interior: Boarding House Kitchen.

Evening. ZULIEKA sorting out some washing. SYBIL is reading a magazine at the table. BERNIE enters, wearing a postman's uniform. SYBIL immediately gets up and goes to leave.

BERNIE: (*Facetiously.*) Goodbye.

SYBIL: I thought you was meant to be looking for another place?

BERNIE: And as soon as I find one, you'll be the first to know.

SYBIL: Glad to hear it.

SYBIL exits.

ZULIEKA: You two got to learn to be in the same room as one another.

BERNIE: It's her.

ZULIEKA: You're as bad as each other. You should talk to her.

BERNIE: What for?

ZULIEKA: Sort it out.

BERNIE: Nothing to sort out. She go chasing after another man. She don't want me. I don't want her.

ZULIEKA: She tell you who this other man is? Her uncle. Sybil's family sent him to persuade her not to marry you. But she wouldn't listen to him. Not until you lost your head. Well, looks like they won. And just whose fault do you suppose that is?

BERNIE: Her...? But... She never say...

FERDY enters – wearing overalls covered in a white dust.

ZULIEKA: Ferdinand, you are filthy!

FERDY: It's only asbestos.

ZULIEKA: I don't know what a man like you is doing working in a factory. Take them off.

FERDY: Not much choice. All I can get is casual job. (*As he takes off his overalls.*) Tell you, I don't know if I can do this much longer. My head aches, my back aches, my legs ache. I hurt all over...

ZULIEKA: Stop feeling so sorry for yourself.

FERDY: That's easy for you to say. You don't have to work. You have money.

ZULIEKA: I don't have to work? Who cleans this place? Who washes your dirty bed linen? Who cooks your breakfast? And I don't have two brass farthings to rub together. I don't own this place. My ex-husband owns it. And he makes me pay him rent way above what I can afford. I have nothing. Let me tell you something, Ferdinand, my father had an accident two years ago. He has been in hospital ever since. And me, his only daughter, I can't afford to get back home to see him. For two years I have been trying to save...for two...

ZULIEKA is close to tears.

FERDY: I'm sorry.

ZULIEKA: Anyway, I thought you was supposed to be going to some university.

FERDY: I am. I will be. When they get in touch. See, when I was back home, two or three year back, I write to tell this professor how much I like his book. He write back say if you are ever in

England don't hesitate to come see me. And so I send a letter the first day I arrive in England say I am here. But he has not contacted me yet.

SYBIL enters. She goes to the sink to rinse out some clothes. FERDY rubs his hands.

ZULIEKA: (*To FERDY.*) Your hands sore?

FERDY: Blisters.

ZULIEKA gets some hand cream.

ZULIEKA: Here… (*She begins rubbing the cream into FERDY's hands.*) Anyway, even if he doesn't get in touch doesn't mean you have to stop writing your book.

FERDY: I have to get a teaching post somewhere. Otherwise no one will want to publish it.

ZULIEKA: I'd like to.

FERDY: You?

ZULIEKA: Yes. Me.

FERDY: Really? Thank you… (*Sudden panic. He looks at BERNIE.*) No! No! Sorry. No…

FERDY jumps up and runs out.

ZULIEKA: Ferdinand! Men!

ZULIEKA exits.

BERNIE: (*In a world of his own.*) Sybil…

SYBIL: What!

BERNIE: Nothing…

WHATEVER HAPPENED

**I didn't mean
To hurt her so
I never loved anyone else
Now I'm in misery
Whatever happened to Sybil and me**

SYBIL: **I loved him ever since I was in school
He used to walk me home and play the fool
I didn't think that it would come to this
To be apart and never share a kiss
Again…**

BERNIE: **We should be together**

Why couldn't I see
Now there isn't a hope
For Sybil and me

SYBIL: We walked hand in hand
Down to the sea
That's all I ever wanted
For Bernie and me

BERNIE/SYBIL: Where did we go wrong
How could it be
Whatever happened

BERNIE: To Sybil and me

BERNIE/SYBIL: Where did we go wrong
How could it be
Whatever happened

SYBIL: To Bernie and me

BERNIE: I shouldn't have done it
How stupid could I be
Now there is no chance
For Sybil and me

SYBIL: We talked through the night
About things we'd agree
It was so simple then
For Bernie and me

BERNIE/SYBIL: Where did we go wrong
How could it be
Whatever happened

BERNIE: To Sybil and me

BERNIE/SYBIL: Where did we go wrong
How could it be
Whatever happened

SYBIL: To Bernie and me

BERNIE/SYBIL: Whatever happened

BERNIE: To Sybil and me

BERNIE/SYBIL: Whatever happened

SYBIL: To Bernie and me

BERNIE/SYBIL: **Whatever happened**…

Song finishes.

Scene 7

Interior: Hospital.

A hospital cubicle. A NURSE fixing a bed. She exits. ADMIRAL enters.

ADMIRAL: (*To audience.*) Accidents will happen.

ADMIRAL exits. LENNIE, in bus conductor's uniform, enters with a limping DENNIS. LENNIE helps DENNIS onto a bed. DENNIS has twisted his ankle.

LENNIE: You okay?

DENNIS: No!

MARY enters.

MARY: How can I help you? (*Sees who it is.*) Oh, it you.

LENNIE: My fren here twiss him ankle.

MARY: (*Calling out.*) Sister!

KATHY enters.

MARY: See what de cat drag in?

KATHY: Well I never. So what happen here?

MARY: Twiss im ankle.

LENNIE: Big fat man in a bowler hat push im off me bus.

DENNIS: Call me all sort a name!

KATHY takes a look at DENNIS' ankle.

DENNIS: (*Screams.*) Yeouchhhh!

MARY: Serious?

KATHY: (*To LENNIE.*) Could you please wait outside?

LENNIE: Bye, Mary.

MARY: Bye bye, Leonard.

LENNIE: You looking nice today.

MARY: Nuff a dat!

LENNIE exits. KATHY continues to examine the leg.

DENNIS: Is it...? What...?

MARY: (*To KATHY.*) Bad news?

KATHY: Better go check we got one a dem wooden leg left.

DENNIS: What!

MARY: Will do.

MARY exits.

KATHY: Don't panic, big boy. Juss a sprain.

DENNIS: No wooden leg?

KATHY: No wooden leg.

DENNIS sighs in relief. KATHY examines his ankle.

KATHY: A lot of ignorant people about.

DENNIS: I couldn't help it.

KATHY: Not you. Man on the bus.

DENNIS: Oh. Yeh. Sorry...

KATHY: You'll need to rest the ankle. Can you take time off work?

DENNIS: What work? Every day I buy the *Evening Standard*, every day I ring up about a job, every time them say 'Come', but when I show up it always the same – 'Sorry, job just gone!' So I say, my brudder he killed in the war. He was in the Royal Air Force – and I show them his medal. But nuttin. No one want to know. Three month now! These people... What I do to them? Every place I go. Everyone I meet. Today, I see these nice banana. So I go in shop to buy me some. The shopkeeper go out back and give me all black banana. I say I don't want black banana. But him say these are the best. But these are bad banana... (*He's cracking up.*) I know banana! What can I do! I know banana... I know banana...

Music cue.

KATHY: My husband was killed in the war. In Tangiers.

DENNIS: Sorry to hear dat...

KATHY: He was a good man. (*Continuing to manipulate the ankle.*) How is that?

DENNIS: (*Dreamily.*) How what?

KATHY: That. Your ankle?

DENNIS: (*Dreamily.*) Ankle...

KATHY: Back in a minute. (*She pecks him on the cheek.*) Don't run away.

KATHY exits. DENNIS is in shock.

MISTER, YOU ARE IN LOVE

DENNIS: (*Touching his face where she kissed him.*) She kiss me... She...
(*Sings.*) **Must resist it, Dennis**
Only make it worse
It must have been a mistake
Must escape from this nurse
Did she really kiss me
Or am I going mad
I wonder if she likes me
Or does she think I'm bad
I can't give in to it
Go fast as I can
Got to get out of here
Got to stand up like a man
Got to get out of here
Got to stand up like a...

DENNIS stands. He has forgotten about his sprained ankle – until he puts his weight on it.

Yaaaaaaaaaa!

DENNIS sits back down again.

(*Weakly.*) **...man**

Lights down – music continues.

Scene 8

Exterior: Piccadilly Circus.

Night. FERDY enters wearing a coat over his work clothes. He is forlorn, perplexed. He gives the statue of Eros a filthy look. He picks up some litter, scrunches it into a ball and throws it at Eros. Eros – played by ADMIRAL – ducks out of the way.

JACQUELINE enters.

JACQUELINE: Looking for someone?

FERDY: (*Jumps with fright.*) No! Stay away from me!

JACQUELINE: I don't bite. Unless you want me to?

FERDY: No! (*Cracking up.*) I don't understand.

JACQUELINE: What don't you understand?

FERDY: You! Women!

JACQUELINE: What do you want to know?

FERDY: I want to know how you know. How you know when it's...she. Her. The one.

JACQUELINE: You mean – Love?
(*Sings.*) **You get goosebumps when she's near?**
You see shooting stars up above?

FERDY: **All of that**

JACQUELINE: **Then, Mister, you are in love**

FERDY: No! I can't be!

JACQUELINE: **You feel knotted in your gut?**
Your heart flutter like a dove?

FERDY: **All of that**

JACQUELINE: **Then, Mister, you are in love**

FERDY: But I can't be!

JACQUELINE: **Don't resist it Mister**
Only make it worse
Don't think it is a mistake
Don't think it is a curse
Got to give in to it
Take it like a man
Got to go and tell her
Got to take her by the hand

FERDY: I can't!

JACQUELINE: Why not?

FERDY: Because... Because... I can't! (*Distraught.*) This isn't happening to me! Tell me it's not happening.

JACQUELINE: **Your head spinning round and round?**

Always get in a huff?

FERDY: **All of that**

JACQUELINE: **Then, Mister, you are in love**

FERDY: No!

JACQUELINE: **You can't look her in the eye?**
And sleep? Can't get enough?

FERDY: **All of that**

JACQUELINE: **Then, Mister, you are in love**

FERDY: I can't be.

JACQUELINE: **Mister, you are in love**

FERDY: No, no, no.

JACQUELINE: **Mister, you are in love**
(*Spoken.*) So do something about it.

Song finishes.

JACQUELINE exits. FERDY sits with his head in his hands.

Blackout.

Scene 9

Interior: Men's Bedroom.

LENNIE enters. He is wearing a coat, hat, gloves and scarf. He is exhausted.

LENNIE: Dennis... Anyone home... (*Checks heater.*) Why dem never buy no paraffin!

There is a knock at the door.

LENNIE: Door open. Come in.

MARY and SYBIL enter.

Music cue.

Yes?

MARY: We was wonderin...could we borrow a lickle cup a shuga?

LENNIE gets some sugar.

SYBIL: You looking tired, Leonard.

MARY: Him have a hard day.

70

SYBIL: Dem working you hard?

MARY: It hard working on de buses.

SYBIL: Big, hard work.

MARY: Big, hard. Make a man all tired an hetup.

SYBIL: (*Encourages MARY to take the initiative.*) You tell him…

WOMAN

MARY: **At de end a de day**
Man need a woman
Make im feel good
Give im all dat she can

SYBIL: **Man need a woman**
Rub im sore back
Make im sigh deep
Make im relax

MARY: **Let me undo you coat** (*She does so.*)
Let me take off you hat (*She does so.*)
Let me show you how
A good woman do dat

SYBIL: **Let me pull off you scarf** (*She does so.*)
Let me take off you glove (*She does so.*)
Let me show you how
A real woman make love

MARY: **You need a woman**

SYBIL: **Spell it!**

MARY: **W-O-M-A-N**

MARY/SYBIL: **You need a woman an you know it**
So you mite jus as well give in

MARY: Sit down, Leonard.

SYBIL: And listen…

MARY: **You need a woman**

SYBIL: **Spell it!**

MARY: **W-O-M-A-N**

SYBIL/MARY: **You need a woman an you know it**
So you mite jus as well give in

MARY: Wassa matta? You is swettin.

SYBIL: Poor Leonard.

MARY: Let me sood you brow.

SYBIL: **Let me undo you jacket** (*She does so.*)
Let me loosen you tie (*She does so.*)
Let me show you how
Man an woman multiply

MARY: **Let me unbutton you shirt** (*She does so.*)
Let me unbuckle you belt (*She does so.*)
Let me do it to you
Let me make you body melt

SYBIL: **You need a woman**

MARY: **Spell it!**

SYBIL: **W-O-M-A-N**

MARY/SYBIL: **You need a woman an you know it**
So you mite jus as well give in

MARY: You lissnin?

SYBIL: **You need a woman**

MARY: **Let me spell it!**
W-O-M-A-N

SYBIL/MARY: **You need a woman an you know it**
So you mite jus as well give in

SYBIL: Let me tell you how it is.

(*Sings.*) **Man need im woman jus like hog need im sow**

SYBIL/MARY: **Man need im woman an wi gonna show you**
how

MARY: You hear me?

(*Sings.*) **Man need im woman jus like rooster need im hen**

MARY/SYBIL: **Man need im woman agen an agen an agen**
You need a woman
Let's spell it!
W-O-M-A-N
Him need a woman an he know it
So him mite jus as well give in

SYBIL: Come on show us what you made of...

MARY: **Touch me**

LENNIE: No!

LENNIE sits on his hands.

MARY/SYBIL: **Touch me**

LENNIE: No!

MARY/SYBIL: **Yes!**

LENNIE: No!

MARY/SYBIL: **Yes!**

LENNIE: No!

MARY/SYBIL: **Yes! Yes!**

LENNIE: **No! No!**

MARY: You breathin heavy, Leonard. You okay?

SYBIL: Ah, look at im trang trang belly. It cute. All sweaty.

MARY: An look at im lickle bellycork. It go – in, out; in, out; in, out...

LENNIE is getting desperate.

Me tink me give im belly a lickle lick licky licky...

MARY leans over him. The door opens. Music stops abruptly. DENNIS is standing in the doorway.

DENNIS: Lennie! What you a do!

LENNIE: Nuttin! I do nuttin!

MARY: Don't worry. Im tell de troot, im do nuttin. Im break no contract. But im will. An soon.

MARY and SYBIL exit. DENNIS stares at LENNIE. LENNIE bursts into tears.

Blackout.

Scene 10

Exterior: Piccadilly Circus.

Day. LENNIE, DENNIS, FERDY and BERNIE sitting worn out and fed up on the steps of Eros as the world passes by. REVEREND enters with his flock. Flock hand the men some leaflets. JACQUELINE enters and crosses to the REVEREND.

JACQUELINE: (*Holding a cigarette.*) Do you have a light?

REVEREND: No!

The REVEREND exits, terrified. JACQUELINE approaches LENNIE, DENNIS, FERDY and BERNIE.

JACQUELINE: What's the matter, boys? Things not working out? Maybe you'll have to rethink that little agreement of yours? How long you got to go? Years, init?

FERDY: Things may not be going exactly to plan, but we're determined not to give in. Isn't that right?

LENNIE/DENNIS/BERNIE: (*Lacklustre.*) Yes.

FERDY: We don't give up just because the going gets a little tough.

JACQUELINE: No time for a drink?

FERDY: No.

JACQUELINE: No time for a woman?

FERDY: No. We have a contact. We all signed it. We're all going to abide by it. Isn't that right? Isn't that right?

LENNIE/DENNIS/BERNIE: (*Lacklustre.*) Yes.

JACQUELINE: You sure about that? Ah well, You know where to find me.

JACQUELINE exits. The men bury their heads in their hands.

EROS: You can't fight it.

FERDY: What?

DENNIS: I didn't say nuttin!

EROS (ADMIRAL) steps down from his plinth.

EROS: You will never get the better of me. I am Eros, son of Aphrodite.

Music cue.

GETTIN HOT

EROS: **You're a lover – Not another**
Not a mother – Nor a brother
No grandmother – Undercover
You're no other – Than a lover

74

Now
You feelin hot – And you can not
Get off the spot – Be a big shot
What you have got – It's not a lot
I tell you what – You have been shot

The men turn around – they've all got arrows in their backs.

EROS: (*Spoken.*) You will never get the better of me. I am Eros, son of Aphrodite.

(*Sings.*) **You are under my power**
I got you under my power
You cannot escape
For you it's far too late

ZULIEKA, MARY, SYBIL and KATHY enter. They look beautiful, gorgeous. They grab the men. A big, exciting and very sexy dance routine choreographed by Eros.

EROS: **Gettin hot – Hot hot hot**
Gettin hot – Hot hot hot
Gettin hot – Hot hot hot
Gettin hot – Hot hot hot

ALL: **Gettin hot – Hot hot hot**
Gettin hot – Hot hot hot
Gettin hot – Hot hot hot
Gettin hot – Hot hot hot
Give it to me
Give it to me
Give it to me
Give it to me

Dance gets even more frenzied.

EROS: You will never get the better of me. I am Eros, son of Aphrodite.

ALL: **Gettin hot – Hot hot hot** (*Et cetera.*)
Yeah!

The women dance off. EROS returns to his plinth. The men return to their positions beneath the statue that they were in prior to the song, their heads buried in their hands.

Song finishes.

EROS fires his arrow.

Blackout. Interval.

ACT TWO

Scene 1

Opening Number: PASS ME BY

MARY and KATHY making beds in the hospital. SYBIL in clouds of steam, working in a laundry. ZULIEKA cleaning the B&B. BERNIE delivering mail. LENNIE up and down the stairs of a double-decker bus. FERDY working in clouds of dust, in an asbestos factory. DENNIS queuing at the Employment Exchange.

PASS ME BY

ALL: *(Except DENNIS.)* **Work work work work**
Work work work work
Work work work

DENNIS: **If you can get it**

They all fall into separate beds.

ALL: *(Except DENNIS.)* **Sleep sleep sleep sleep**
Sleep sleep sleep sleep
Sleep sleep sleep

DENNIS: **If you can get some**

They all jump out of bed.

ALL: *(Except DENNIS.)* **Work work work work**
Work work work work
Work work work

DENNIS: **If you can get it**

They all fall into separate beds.

ALL: *(Except DENNIS.)* **Sleep sleep sleep sleep**
Sleep sleep sleep sleep
Sleep sleep sleep

DENNIS: **If you can get some**

They all jump out of bed.

LENNIE: **I get up**
MARY: **I'm all messed**
BERNIE: **I get dressed**
SYBIL: **I detest**
FERDY: **Got bad chest**

76

KATHY: **Got no zest**
DENNIS: **Got no vest**
ZULIEKA: **A new test**

They work.

BERNIE: **I go work**
SYBIL: **Get depressed**
DENNIS: **It's no jest**
ZULIEKA: **I'm not blessed**
LENNIE: **Second best**
MARY: **I get stressed**
FERDY: **Get obsessed**
KATHY: **Never guessed**

They return to their beds.

FERDY: **I go bed**
SYBIL: **Get underssed**
LENNIE: **Get depressed**
ZULIEKA: **I can't rest**
BERNIE: **Can't digest**
MARY: **This unrest**
DENNIS: **Get all messed**
KATHY: **Overstressed**

ALL: **I feel so fed up**
   Live a lie
   I feel so lonely
   I could cry
   And all the time
   Days pass me by
   All the time
   Life pass me by
   Just pass me by

ALL: (*Except DENNIS.*) **Work work work work**
   Work work work work
   Work work work

DENNIS: **If you can get it**

They all fall into separate beds.

ALL: (*Except DENNIS.*) **Sleep sleep sleep sleep**
   Sleep sleep sleep sleep
   Sleep sleep sleep

DENNIS: **If you can get some**

77

ALL: (*Except DENNIS.*) **Work work work work**
Work work work work
Work work work

DENNIS: **If you can get it**

They all fall into separate beds.

ALL: (*Except DENNIS.*) **Sleep sleep sleep sleep**
Sleep sleep sleep sleep
Sleep sleep sleep

DENNIS: **If you can get some**

ALL: (*Except DENNIS.*) **Work work work work**
Work work work work
Work work work work
Work work work work

DENNIS: I want to go home...

Blackout.

Scene 2

Interior: Boarding House Kitchen.

LENNIE and DENNIS playing dominoes, BERNIE, SYBIL, MARY and KATHY are all trying to cook at the same time. FERDY trying to read. ZULIEKA attempting to sweep the floor.

BERNIE: (*Grabs a saucepan from SYBIL.*) I was going to use that.

SYBIL: Get off.

BERNIE: Give it –

SYBIL: It's my time now!

BERNIE: I had to work late!

FERDY: Would you please be quiet?

ZULIEKA: Excuse me...

KATHY: (*To DENNIS and LENNIE.*) Can you move, please?

DENNIS: We busy.

KATHY: Please clear the table.

DENNIS: We playing dominoes!

ZULIEKA: Excuse me...

SYBIL: (*Still playing tug-o-war with the pan.*) Give it to me. Postman!

BERNIE: Get off. Washerwoman!

FERDY: I'm trying to read.

MARY: Whose turn put a shilling in the meter?

LENNIE: Don't look at me.

MARY: When you last put a shilling in?

LENNIE: I put my shilling in!

KATHY: Right!

KATHY clears away the dominoes.

LENNIE: What you do you frumpy old bat!

KATHY: What did you call me!

MARY: What did you call her!

SYBIL: Give it to me!

ZULIEKA: Excuse me...

BERNIE: I will not.

SYBIL pulls at the pan BERNIE is holding. BERNIE drops it, spilling the contents over the floor.

Music cue.

BERNIE: You stupid woman.

SYBIL: You pathetic man.

BETTER THAN YOU

BERNIE: **If there's one thing I can't stand
It's a clumsy, stupid woman**

SYBIL: **If there's one thing I can't stand
It's a rude, pathetic man**

MARY/KATHY/SYBIL: **Get out of our way**
BERNIE/LENNIE/DENNIS: **You've got a nerve**
MARY/KATHY/SYBIL: **Do what we say**
BERNIE/LENNIE/DENNIS: **Get what you deserve**

MARY/KATHY/SYBIL: **You're out of your mind**
BERNIE/LENNIE/DENNIS: **Oh is that right**
MARY/KATHY/SYBIL: **So stick to your kind**

BERNIE/LENNIE/DENNIS: **You started this fight**

MARY/KATHY/SYBIL: **That just is not true**
BERNIE/LENNIE/DENNIS: **You're full of hot air**
MARY/KATHY/SYBIL: **We're all sick of you**
BERNIE/LENNIE/DENNIS: **As if we care**

MARY/KATHY/SYBIL: **You're hopeless and dim**
BERNIE/LENNIE/DENNIS: **You haven't a clue**
MARY/KATHY/SYBIL: **Can't do anything**
BERNIE/LENNIE/DENNIS: **We're better than you**
MARY/KATHY/SYBIL: **We're better than you**
BERNIE/LENNIE/DENNIS: **We're better than you**
MARY/KATHY/SYBIL: **We're better than you**
BERNIE/LENNIE/DENNIS: **We're better than you**

LENNIE: You can't play cricket, you can't play cards, you can't drink –

MARY: Can't – !

(*Sings.*) **I can drink more than you**
LENNIE: **Would you listen to dat**
MARY: **Still be standin too**
LENNIE: **An I eat my hat**

MARY opens a cupboard and takes out a bottle of rum and two glasses. She places the glasses on the table and fills them.

FERDY: Abstinence, Lennie. Remember our pledge.

KATHY: Mary…

MARY: I'm doing this in the cause of science.

LENNIE: Me too. Drink!

MARY and LENNIE down the rum in one go. LENNIE refills the glasses.

LENNIE: Drink!

They down the rum in one go. MARY refills the glasses. They continue to drink, matching each other shot for shot throughout the rest of the scene.

MARY/KATHY/SYBIL: **We're better than you**
BERNIE/LENNIE/DENNIS: **We're better than you**
MARY/KATHY/SYBIL: **We're better than you**
BERNIE/LENNIE/DENNIS: **We're better than you**

SYBIL: You can't cook, you can't talk in words of more than one syllable, you can't dance –

BERNIE: Can't –

(Sings.) **I dance better than you**
SYBIL: **That just is not true**
BERNIE: **Got fast shuffle-shoe**
SYBIL: **Like a fat kangaroo**

BERNIE: **Tell you how you dance**
SYBIL: **Tell you how you dance**
BERNIE: **You wiggle and prance**
SYBIL: **Like your pants full of ants**

BERNIE/LENNIE/DENNIS: **We're better than you**
MARY/KATHY/SYBIL: **We're better than you**
BERNIE/LENNIE/DENNIS: **We're better than you**
MARY/KATHY/SYBIL: **We're better than you**

BERNIE and SYBIL begin a competitive dance sequence – getting ever more daring and spectacular as they try to out-do each other.

KATHY: Why is it men always have to be so competitive? Why can't they do something useful?

DENNIS: What you mean 'useful'?

KATHY: What I say – useful. Like caring for people.

DENNIS: Like knittin?

KATHY: Knittin? Yes, if you like. Knittin!

DENNIS: I can knit.

KATHY: You!

DENNIS: *(Sings.)* **Knit faster than you**
KATHY: **The man's off his head**
DENNIS: **Knit scarf an glove too**
KATHY: **I knit my bedspread**

DENNIS: **Knit my socks and my hat**
KATHY: **Just stay where you sat**

KATHY gets some wool and knitting needles from a cupboard.

DENNIS: **Knit faster than you**
KATHY: **We see about that**

KATHY hands some wool and needles to DENNIS.

KATHY: Ready... Set... Knit!

KATHY and DENNIS knit frenziedly.

MARY/KATHY/SYBIL: **We're better than you**
BERNIE/LENNIE/DENNIS: **We're better than you**
MARY/KATHY/SYBIL: **We're better than you**
BERNIE/LENNIE/DENNIS: **We're better than you**

FERDY: Women!

ZULIEKA: You have something to say?

FERDY: Sometimes women can be so...ridiculous.

ZULIEKA: It's you that's ridiculous!

FERDY: Me!

(Sings.) **I've written a book**
ZULIEKA: **So let's take a look**

FERDY: **It's not finished yet**
ZULIEKA: **Not started I bet**

FERDY: **I'm cleverer than you**
ZULIEKA: **So what's your IQ?**

FERDY: **Above average**
ZULIEKA: **I speak six language**
  Girls clev'rer than boys
FERDY: **They just make more noise**

ZULIEKA: **Have higher IQ**
FERDY: **I don't think that's true**

WOMEN: **We're better than you**
MEN: **We're better than you**
WOMEN: **We're better than you**
MEN: **We're better than you**

*A stand-off between FERDY and ZULIEKA. BERNIE and
SYBIL collapse from their exertions. DENNIS and KATHY
measure what they have knitted – it's about the same.*

MARY: *(Drunk.)* Drink!

LENNIE and MARY drink. LENNIE sets up two more shots.

LENNIE: *(Drunk.)* Drink!

*LENNIE and MARY drink. They sway then collapse simul-
taneously into the arms of DENNIS and SYBIL respectively.
DENNIS and BERNIE carry LENNIE off. KATHY and
SYBIL carry MARY off.*

Song finishes.

FERDY: You smell something?

ZULIEKA rushes to the oven and pulls out a singed dinner.

Blackout.

Scene 3

Interior: University Building.

*A SECRETARY sits typing at her desk outside an office. She is concentrating
hard on her work and does not notice FERDY when he enters. FERDY
waits for a while for her to acknowledge him, but she doesn't realise he is
there.*

FERDY: Excuse me.

The SECRETARY screams with surprise.

FERDY: Sorry! Sorry! Sorry! I didn't mean to... I'm sorry. I have
come to see the professor.

SECRETARY: Is he expecting you?

FERDY: No, you see he wrote to me a while ago, to say if ever I am
in England... I sent a letter a few months ago to say here I am,
but I don't hear anything, so I thought maybe if I drop by.
This...

Takes out his letter from the professor.

Look, look, you see...from the professor...

The SECRETARY looks at the letter.

FERDY: I didn't mean to give you a fright...

SECRETARY: The professor is a very busy man.

FERDY: I appreciate that...

SECRETARY: Wait there.

FERDY: Thank you.

*The SECRETARY takes FERDY's letter and exits into the office.
FERDY waits nervously. He picks up a large pencil sharpener;
he turns it upside down to look at the bottom and the shavings
spill out everywhere. He tries desperately to clean up. The
SECRETARY re-enters.*

SECRETARY: I'm afraid the professor can't see you now.

FERDY: I can come back later.

SECRETARY: He's very busy.

FERDY: Tomorrow, then? Or next week?

SECRETARY: The professor has a very heavy schedule.

FERDY: Any time.

SECRETARY: I'm afraid he really can't spare any time at the
moment.

FERDY: But him say –

SECRETARY: I won't tell you again.

FERDY: I have a letter –

SECRETARY: You really must learn to know your place, young
man!

FERDY exits. The SECRETARY goes to her desk intercom.

SECRETARY: (*Into intercom.*) He's gone.

Blackout.

Scene 4

Interior: B&B Men's Bedroom.

FERDY enters, dejected. He sits on his bed.

THE PRICE WE PAY

FERDY: **Hope, all I ever had was hope**
That I would be someone
Do something
Get somewhere
Dreams, all I ever had were dreams
That I would reach the top
Make my mark
Never stop

But hope is shattered
Nothing seems
Like it ever mattered
In broken dreams
For having hope
This is the price we pay
For having dreams
This is the price we pay

Faith, all I ever had was faith
That I would be someone
Do something
Get somewhere
Trust, all I ever showed was trust
I could be relied upon
Always there
Never gone
But faith is shattered
Nothing spoken
Like it never mattered
When trust is broken
For having faith
This is the price we pay
For having trust
This is the price we pay
For having hope
This is the price we pay
For having dreams
This is the price we pay
This is the price we pay

Song finishes.

FERDY takes out a pen and some paper. He has made a decision. He starts to write something...

Lights down.

Scene 5

Exterior: Piccadilly Circus.

Underscore: YOU DO IT.

Smog – yellowish-green, thick and heavy, a pea-souper. Saturday afternoon.

ADMIRAL and JACQUELINE on the steps of Eros. REVEREND enters with KATHY. KATHY exits. REVEREND is approached by a SHADY-LOOKING MAN. FERDY enters. ZULIEKA, SYBIL and MARY enter, they have been shopping. FERDY takes ADMIRAL to one side and hands him a letter; he whispers something into ADMIRAL'S ear and gives him some money. ZULIEKA, SYBIL and MARY exit. The ADMIRAL follows them off. A PEDESTRIAN bumps into REVEREND and exits. The SHADY-LOOKING MAN exits. REVEREND realizes he has been pick-pocketed. JACQUELINE crosses to him.

JACQUELINE: You okay? Hey, mister…

The REVEREND turns round to see who it is.

JACQUELINE: Oh, it's you.

The REVEREND searches his pockets again.

JACQUELINE: You lost something?

REVEREND: This… A man…he was asking for directions. Some-one bumped into me. I didn't see who it was. My wallet… All my money…Gone!

JACQUELINE: Pick-pocket.

REVEREND: Why me? I tell you, if I get my hands on that…that…

JACQUELINE: Shouldn't you turn the other cheek or something?

REVEREND: How am I going to get home? I haven't got a penny.

JACQUELINE takes out some money and offers it to him.

REVEREND: No.

JACQUELINE: Take it.

REVEREND: Certainly not.

JACQUELINE: Take the money.

REVEREND: This reminds me of the story of the Good Samaritan. One day –

JACQUELINE: Stop! Take it before I change my mind.

The REVEREND takes the money.

REVEREND: Thank you.

JACQUELINE: It's no problem.

REVEREND: I'll pay you back.

JACQUELINE: Whenever.

REVEREND exits. FERDY is pacing nervously, stopping inter-mittently to look at his watch. DENNIS enters. They did not expect to see each other.

FERDY: Dennis.

DENNIS: Ferdy.

FERDY: So you're...?

DENNIS: Er... Me a come feed de pidgin.

FERDY: Me too.

An uneasy silence.

FERDY: Well, can't stand about all day...

DENNIS: No.

FERDY: Right. Well. I'll be...

DENNIS: Yes.

FERDY moves away. When DENNIS isn't looking he slips out of sight behind Eros. ADMIRAL re-enters.

Pischt! Admiral! Ova here!

ADMIRAL: What you want?

DENNIS: Some advice...about...

ADMIRAL: Woman?

DENNIS: (*Looking around nervously.*) Sssssh! Not so loud.

ADMIRAL: Five pound!

DENNIS: Okay, you win.

He pays up.

I need to know...You know...What I do?

ADMIRAL: First of all – your hat.

DENNIS: My hat?

ADMIRAL: You wear it like dis...

Adjusts DENNIS' hat.

Like an awning over the love shop of your eyes. Next your arms – cross over you belly like a rabbit on a spit...

Shows him.

Or your hand in your pocket like a man in dem old paintin. Casual.

Shows him.

Den... You muss have a song.

DENNIS: A song?

ADMIRAL: You must have a tune at the tip of your tongue, a sweet, hummingbird melody. You move to it slowly, give it meaning with turning up your eyelid, sigh a note, and sing a note, sometime through the troat as if you swallow love, sometime through the nose as if you sniff up love by smelling it. And not too long in one tune, but a snip and away. Dis, to woman, is the greatess compliment you can pay, dis will have a woman betray her feelin who would never do dis, dis will make you in her eye a man of substance, dis, I tell you, is the very essence of love. Do you note me?

DENNIS: A song.

ADMIRAL: What her name?

DENNIS: Kathy.

ADMIRAL: I have juss the song for you.

DENNIS: How it go?

ADMIRAL: Two an six.

DENNIS: Two an six?

ADMIRAL: Such is the price of love.

DENNIS: Man, me still have to pay off me fare to come to Inglan!

ADMIRAL: The choice is yours.

DENNIS: (*Pays up.*) Betta be good.

ADMIRAL: Okay. Repeat after me.

Plays his guitar.
(*Sings.*) **When I look into your eyes
I see paradise**

DENNIS: **When I look into your eyes
I see paradise**

ADMIRAL: **When you put your hand in mine
I can feel the sunshine**

88

DENNIS: **When you put your hand in mine**
I can feel the sunshine

ADMIRAL: **When we walk upon the sand**
I think I understand

DENNIS: **When we walk upon the sand**
I think I understand

ADMIRAL: **When I kiss...**

(*Spoken.*) What name again?

DENNIS: Kathy.

ADMIRAL: **When I kiss Kathy beneath the coconut tree**
I want to sing...

DENNIS: **When I kiss Kathy beneath the coconut tree**
I want to sing...

ADMIRAL: **Is it love love love**

(*Spoken.*) Sing wid me

ADMIRAL/DENNIS: **Is it love love love**
Is it love love love
Is it love love love
That I am feeling
Oh-oh-oh

LENNIE: (*Voice off.*) Admiral... Admiral...

DENNIS: Sssshhh! Ssshh!

ADMIRAL stops playing.

LENNIE: (*Voice off.*) Admiral...

DENNIS: You tell no one bout dis. You hear? No one!

DENNIS dashes behind a vendor's stall as LENNIE enters.

LENNIE: Who dat you sing with?

ADMIRAL: Just me here.

LENNIE: (*Hands him a fiver.*) You won the bet. But you tell no one bout dis. Got it?

ADMIRAL: I got it. So who de lucky girl?

LENNIE: Mary. Tell you, I never felt like dis before.

ADMIRAL: And what you plan to do?

LENNIE: I don't know yet.

ADMIRAL: You need a song.

LENNIE: A song! Yes!

ADMIRAL: Five shillin.

LENNIE: Five sh-! You rob me!

LENNIE pays up.

ADMIRAL: Sing after me.

Plays his guitar.
(*Sings.*) **When I look into your eyes
I see paradise**

LENNIE: **When I look into your eyes
I see paradise**

BERNIE: (*Voice off.*) Admiral!

ADMIRAL stops playing. They listen.

BERNIE: (*Voice off.*) Admiral! That you?

LENNIE: You keep your mout close bout this. Firm close shut!

LENNIE dashes out of sight behind a parked car. BERNIE enters.

BERNIE: Admiral...

ADMIRAL: Five pound.

BERNIE: (*Handing over a fiver.*) How did you know?

ADMIRAL: Let us call it intuition.

BERNIE: It's Sybil... I have to find a way to get her back.

ADMIRAL: You need a song.

BERNIE: Of course!

ADMIRAL: Seven an six.

BERNIE: What!

ADMIRAL: Sing afta me...

Music cue.

LENNIE leaps out.

You Do It

LENNIE: **You do it – I knew it
You blew it – I knew it
Who do it? – You do it
You undo it – You adieu it**

90

You askew it – You kazoo it
Barbecue it – In a stew it
I knew it would be you – Bernie
Bernie and im trickery
What happen it just have to be
It is such a tragedy
A comedy, go tweedle-deedle-dee
His laxity is catastrophy
No amnesty for this infancy
Im fidgety, an panicky
An garlicky, that poor Bernie

BERNIE: **It's true**
I'm not like you
What could I do
I'm in love

LENNIE: A good thing I a man of my word.

DENNIS leaps out.

DENNIS: **You do it – I knew it**
You blew it – I knew it
Who do it? – You do it
You undo it – You adieu it
You askew it – You kazoo it
Barbecue it – In a stew it
I knew it would be you – Bernie and Lennie

BERNIE: (*To LENNIE.*) You?

DENNIS: I hear him tell the Admiral bout Mary.

Mimicking LENNIE.

'A good thing I am a man of my word'

(*Sings.*) **Lennie an im honesty**
In agony an ecstasy
Wat im say is fantasy
You mus agree dis is treachery
So blatantly it maggoty
Lovey dovey got a flat batt'ry
Now im crotchety an finickity
In misery, dat poor Lennie

LENNIE: **It's true**
I'm not like you
What could I do

I'm in love

FERDY leaps out.

FERDY: **You do it – I knew it**
You blew it – I knew it
Who do it? – You do it
You undo it – You adieu it
You askew it – You kazoo it
Barbecue it – In a stew it
I knew it would be you – Bernie, Lennie and Dennis

LENNIE: (*To DENNIS.*) Dennis!

FERDY: (*Quoting DENNIS.*) 'When I kiss Kathy beneath the coconut tree…'

(*Sings.*) **Dennis an Im Judas kiss**
This artifice I now dismiss
And expose this hypothesis
From genesis to nemesis
The precipice to the abyss
We'll reminisce this cowardice
With emphasis on what's amiss
It's come to this, for poor Dennis

ADMIRAL: Ferdy –

FERDY: Not now.

DENNIS: **It's true**
I'm not like you
What could I do
I'm in love

FERDY: And I thought you were all determined not to give in.

ADMIRAL: Ferdy –

FERDY: Not now. Seems I'm the only one with any willpower around here.

ADMIRAL: Me get a lickle confuse…

FERDY: Not now.

ADMIRAL: (*Producing FERDY's letter.*) The lady you ask me give this letter, she call what?

BERNIE snatches the letter.

FERDY: That's private.

BERNIE: (*Reads the letter.*) 'My dearest darling Zulieka, I can take this no longer. I am a fool. From the moment I saw you, my heart was yours. The past months have been agony. Zulieka, I love you.'

LENNIE/DENNIS: What!

FERDY: **It's true**
I'm just like you
What could I do
I'm in love

MEN: **We do it – We knew it**
We blew it – We knew it
Who do it? – We do it
We undo it – We adieu it
We askew it – We kazoo it
Barbecue it – In a stew it
We knew it would not be easy

Song finishes.

DENNIS: So now what we a do?

ADMIRAL: Let me tell you –

LENNIE: I think we've had enough of your advice.

FERDY: Make everyone pay for the same tune. I think you better reimburse these boys!

BERNIE: Im what!

DENNIS: Yeh, man.

LENNIE: Pay up!

ADMIRAL: Cha!

ADMIRAL pays back the money for the song.

FERDY: Come...

ADMIRAL: Let me give you –

FERDY: We don't need your help.

FERDY, LENNIE, DENNIS and BERNIE exit.

ADMIRAL: Don't need my help... We see about dat...

Blackout.

93

Scene 6

Interior: Boarding House Kitchen

ZULIEKA, SYBIL, MARY and KATHY sit around the table. The table is piled with gifts: chocolates, flowers, jewellery, et cetera.

MARY: So what you got?

KATHY: I got a scarf and a hat.

SYBIL: I got perfume. Say Chanel, but... (*Sniffs.*) Don't smell much like it.

ZULIEKA: (*To MARY.*) And what is that?

MARY: A sugar mouse. What you?

ZULIEKA: I have a pearl necklace and a long... (*Unfolds a piece of paper.*) ...long... (*Continues to unfold the piece of paper.*) ...long poem.

MARY: Shame the necklace not longer and the poem shorter.

KATHY: Why must they insist on remaining anonymous?

SYBIL: Can't be seen to be breaking their oath.

MARY: Damn fool idea.

ZULIEKA: You have to admit they have been working hard.

MARY: True.

ZULIEKA: At least they try to make something of themselves.

KATHY: They're not all bad.

SYBIL: No.

A knock at the door.

MARY: I'll go.

MARY exits.

ZULIEKA: What flowers did you get?

KATHY: Roses and chrysanthemums. You?

ZULIEKA: Lilies and anemones.

SYBIL: Original. I had roses. A dozen. Red.

ZULIEKA: Same as Mary.

KATHY: I think maybe Hyde Park be a bit short of blooms this year.

MARY enters with ADMIRAL.

MARY: It's Admiral, come for the pardner money.

ADMIRAL: Ladies, how are you this fine evening? Look like you have some admirer?

MARY: Mmm hmm. And you never guess who?

ADMIRAL: Oh, me got a good idea. I overhear them and... No, I can't...

KATHY: Can't what?

ADMIRAL: I overheard... No...

MARY: Spit it out!

ADMIRAL: I think they are up to something.

SYBIL: Such as?

ADMIRAL: A trick of some kind. I heard them talking bout a club or something?

KATHY: I got a note. You?

MARY: Mmm hum.

SYBIL: And me.

ZULIEKA: A poem – and a note. From my 'anonymous admirer'.

KATHY: Why can't they just put their name?

SYBIL: Because maybe they are up to something.

MARY: What yours say?

KATHY: (*Reading from her note.*) Meet me tonight at the Circus. The Zanzibar Club. And all will be revealed.

SYBIL: Me too. All will be revealed. Just meet me tonight at the Zanzibar Club in Piccadilly Circus.

MARY: Same. Meet me tonight at the Circus. And all will be revealed.

ZULIEKA: Well, surprise, surprise – Meet me tonight...

WOMEN: ...at the circus. And all will be revealed.

ADMIRAL: So, you go?

Music cue.

SYBIL: What if it is a trick?

MARY: You mean a set-up?

ZULIEKA: This could be one of their little games.

SYBIL: Make us think they've fallen for us, then…

ZULIEKA: (*Imitating FERDY's voice.*) 'Ha ha ha – You fell for it!'

KATHY: Make us look fools.

SYBIL: I wouldn't put is past them.

MARY: Having a laugh.

KATHY: And the joke's on us!

Meet Me Tonight At the Circus

KATHY: **I've come a long long way**
Been a struggle to get where I'm at today

MARY: **Been one hell of a fight**
Didn't get no quick fix over night

ZULIEKA: **Then along come a man**
With some flowers in his hand

SYBIL: **Expect you to drop all**
Just because he give that big boy tarzan call

(*Spoken.*) I don't want to make the same mistake again.

MARY: You're right. We shouldn't rush into this.

KATHY: Let's think about it.

ZULIEKA: Ever meet a man didn't turn out to be a good-for-nothing, lustful, liar…

(*Sings.*) **We don't want to jump out the frying pan**

WOMEN: **Into the fire**

SYBIL: **Think they can click their fingers**

ZULIEKA: **And we come running**

MARY: **Sugar and cheap perfume**

KATHY: **And the world a wonderful place**

SYBIL: **Think we'll go weak-kneed**

MARY: **When they come gunning**

ZULIEKA: **Think we'll be so grateful**

KATHY: **Put us in our place**

SYBIL: **Think we change our mind**
When life get too much grind

MARY: **Soon as them click their finger**

KATHY: **Dirty look if we malinger**

ZULIEKA: Remember…

(*Sings.*) **Six month ago them say they gonna shirk us**

WOMEN: **Now it's, meet me tonight at the circus**

KATHY: **Six month ago too busy them hard workers**

WOMEN: **Now it's, meet me tonight at the circus**

SYBIL: **Six month ago women are the worst curse**

WOMEN: **Now it's, meet me tonight at the circus**

MARY: **Six month ago them fighting us like ghurkas**

WOMEN: **Now it's, meet me tonight at the circus**
Meet me tonight at the circus
Meet me tonight at the circus

Song finishes.

ADMIRAL: Maybe you should play them at their own game

ZULIEKA: How do you mean?

ADMIRAL: I have an idea…

(*To audience.*) Well, what did you expect…plain sailing? I don't tink so…

Blackout.

Scene 7

Interior: Zanzibar Club.

Night. ADMIRAL is performing in a dark, seedy, underground club. Four unidentifiable figures are sitting in the corner of a number of darkened booths. We don't know it yet but these figures are ZULIEKA disguised as SYBIL, SYBIL disguised as ZULIEKA, MARY disguised as KATHY, and KATHY disguised as MARY. A few other drinkers at the bar. FERDY, BERNIE, LENNIE, and DENNIS enter.

DENNIS: Man, it a bit dark.

FERDY: You see them anywhere?

SYBIL: (*Dangling ZULIEKA's pearls from out of the darkness for FERDY to see.*) Yoo-hoo... Ferdy...

FERDY: Zulieka? That you?

FERDY steps closer.

SYBIL: Not so close! Wait!

ZULIEKA: (*Dangling her perfumed wrist from the darkness for BERNIE to smell.*) Bernie...

BERNIE: Sybil?

KATHY: (*Dangling MARY's sugar mouse from the darkness.*) Leonard...

LENNIE: (*Steps forward.*) Mary!

KATHY: Stop right where you are!

MARY: (*Waving KATHY's scarf into the light.*) Oh, Dennis...

DENNIS: K-K-K-Kathy...

SYBIL: So what is it you boys want to say?

FERDY: Zulieka, I want to tell you... You see...

ADMIRAL strums the introduction to Is It Love.

FERDY: (*Sings – to SYBIL, thinking it's ZULIEKA.*)

When I look into your eyes
I see paradise

SYBIL: Ferdinand, I never knew.

LENNIE: (*Sings – to KATHY thinking it's MARY.*)

When you put your hand in mine
I can feel the sunshine

KATHY: Is that true, Leonard?

BERNIE: (*Sings – to ZULIEKA thinking it's SYBIL.*)

When we walk upon the sand
I want to hold your hand

ZULIEKA: Bernie, that's lovely.

DENNIS: (*Sings – to MARY thinking it's KATHY.*)

When we kiss beneath the coconut tree

MARY: Dennis!

DENNIS: **I want to sing...**

MEN: **Is it love love love**
  Is it love love love
  Is it love love love
  That I am feeling
  Oh-oh-oh

The women come dancing out of the shadows.

MEN: **Is it love... love... love...**

ADMIRAL stops playing. The men realise they've been singing to the wrong woman – they are in shock.

FERDY: Sybil?

SYBIL: That's right.

BERNIE: But?

ZULIEKA: Zulieka. Who did you think I was?

LENNIE: Where's?

MARY: Over here, Leonard.

DENNIS: M-M-M-M-M-M-M-M...

KATHY: Something wrong Dennis?

ZULIEKA: You boys certainly know how to make a simple thing complicated.

FERDY: Oh no...

DENNIS: I don't...

FERDY: Oh no...

DENNIS: My head's hurting.

BERNIE: Sybil...

LENNIE: You mean, I was...with that dowdy, frigid, frumpy...

Music cue.

KATHY: I just about had enough of you, cap-i-tan!

AIN'T NOTHING HOTTER

KATHY: Let me tell you something...

(Sings.) **Give you a surprise**

When I married before
My man always satisfied

LENNIE: Oh yeh?

KATHY: **A good married couple**
One woman, one man
Know each other's bodies
Like the back of their hand

LENNIE: So?

KATHY: **They relax with each other**
Know how to please
Give themself completely
All inhibition release
Cos there ain't nothing hotter
Than a good, upstanding
God fearing, respectable woman
Let me tell you

LENNIE: Pigs might fly!

KATHY: **A good married couple**
Need no straying eye
Got all that they need
To love and satisfy
They know how to touch
To stroke and to squeeze
They know what to whisper
Beg for mercy if they please
Cos there ain't nothing hotter
Than a good, upstanding
God fearing, respectable woman
Let me tell you
There ain't no one sexier
Than a good, upstanding
God fearing respectable woman
Let me tell you

KATHY dances seductively. She is good – and very sexy.

KATHY: Wassa matta, bwoys – you looking a lickle hot under de collar...Still think I'm dowdy? Still think I don't know what to do wid it?

DENNIS: No...

LENNIE: I...I...I...

KATHY: **We do it when we wake up**
We do it with our cornflakes
We do it for elevenses
We do it during lunch break
We do it in the evening
We do it with our coco
We do it all the time
And everywhere we go-go
Cos there ain't nothing hotter
Than a good, upstanding
God fearing, respectable woman
Telling you
There ain't no one sexier
Than a good, upstanding
God fearing respectable woman
Let me tell you

The men are in a state of shock.

KATHY: You want to know the secret of great s.e.x. – find yourself a good woman...and marry her. Then you find out what loving is *really* all about. You don't know what you missing, big bwoys!

KATHY blows the men a kiss. They fall over.

Song finishes.

The women exit.

ADMIRAL: Don't look at me...

Lights down.

Scene 8

Interior: Boarding House Kitchen.

ZULIEKA, SYBIL, MARY and KATHY celebrating their success in duping the men.

ZULIEKA: Poor Bernie, he really did seem quite put out.

SYBIL: What a lamentable bunch! I thought Ferdy was going to burst into tears any second!

MARY: Oh boy, the look on their faces!

KATHY: Priceless!

A door closes off-stage.

MARY: Them!

KATHY: What we do?

SYBIL: Carry on as we left off.

ZULIEKA: Play the innocent.

FERDY, BERNIE, LENNIE and DENNIS enter.

BERNIE: We need to talk.

FERDY: We've been foolish.

MARY: True.

BERNIE: Please, Sybil. I'll do anything.

ZULIEKA: Hold on, half an hour ago you wanted to hold my hand!

BERNIE: No, no, no. Please, can we stop this?

DENNIS: Kathy...

KATHY: I thought it was Mary you was interested in?

MARY: It is.

DENNIS: No, not you. I don't like you.

MARY: Huh!

KATHY: You don't like my friend?

DENNIS: I love your friend.

KATHY: You love her!

DENNIS: No!

LENNIE: (*To MARY.*) It's me! I love you!

MARY: Make your minds up.

SYBIL: Hold Bernie up, someone. He looks like he's going to faint.

FERDY: Please, you've had your laugh. You've made us look the fools we are. I can't take this any longer.

ZULIEKA: Enough of this. I'm tired. I'm off to bed.

FERDY: No! Please! We have gone against our word for you.

ZULIEKA: I've had enough of your games, Ferdy.

FERDY: Games! I've never been more serious!

MARY: You mean to say all the gifts and letters weren't just a set up?

MEN: No!

LENNIE: We're serious!

DENNIS: Serious!

ZULIEKA: How can we be sure?

FERDY: Please, believe us. Please, please, please... Zulieka, I am beggin you... I don't know if I can go on... I...

Falls sobbing to his knees.

I will do anythin...anythin... Oh Zulieka, please...

Music cue.

Please, Please, Please Take Me Seriously

FERDY: **Whatever you want**
I well agree

ZULIEKA: That so?

FERDY: **Please, please, please take me seriously**

MEN **Please, please, please take us seriously**

FERDY: **Whatever you crave**
Whatever you need

ZULIEKA: Really?

FERDY: **Please, please, please take me seriously**

MEN **Please, please, please take us seriously**

FERDY: **It was wrong what I did**
My regret's plain to see

ZULIEKA: Uh huh...

FERDY: **Please, please, please take me seriously**

MEN: **Please, please, please take us seriously**

FERDY: **I've broken my word**
And that's painful for me

ZULIEKA: Oh yes?

FERDY: **Please, please, please take me seriously**

MEN: **Please, please, please take us seriously**

ZULIEKA: How can we when you spent the last six months telling us you don't need us? No, no.

    (*Sings.*) **The things that you say**
    Are hard to believe

FERDY: It's the truth!

ZULIEKA: **How can I**
    Take you seriously

WOMEN: **How can we**
    Take you seriously

ZULIEKA: **You say you repent**
    But words come cheaply

FERDY: I mean it!

ZULIEKA: **How can I**
    Take you seriously

WOMEN: **How can we**
    Take you seriously

ZULIEKA: **You make promises**
    You likely won't keep

FERDY: I will!

ZULIEKA: **How can I**
    Take you seriously

WOMEN: **How can we**
    Take you seriously

ZULIEKA: **Think you can buy us**
    But it's not that easy

FERDY: Zulieka, please…

ZULIEKA: **How can I**
    Take you seriously

WOMEN: **How can we**
    Take you seriously

MEN **Please, please, please take us seriously**

WOMEN: **How can we**
Take you seriously

MEN: **Please, please, please take us seriously**

WOMEN: **How can we**
Take you seriously

MEN: **Please, please, please take us seriously**
Please, please, please take us seriously

FERDY: Pleeeeeeeeeeeeeeeeeeeeease!

Song finishes.

FERDY: Zulieka... Please... Just tell me what to do...

ZULIEKA: Okay, listen. I want you carry on with your agreement. If, after one year, you still want me, then we'll see.

FERDY: A whole year?

ZULIEKA: What I said.

BERNIE: And what about me?

SYBIL: If you want me back – you will do as Ferdy...and I want you to spend all your spare time doing volunteer work in a hospital.

KATHY: Fine idea!

SYBIL: For one year. Then...maybe...

DENNIS: And what about me, my love? My...wife?

KATHY: A year. Then we'll see.

DENNIS: I swear I will do this.

LENNIE: Mary...

MARY: Twelve months.

LENNIE: I...I...don't know if...I...I...

ZULIEKA: Well, well, well, looks like they are serious after all...

You Do It (Reprise.)

WOMEN: **You do it – We knew it**
You blew it – We knew it
Who do it? – You do it
You undo it – You adieu it
You askew it – You kazoo it

105

PAUL SIRETT

Barbecue it – In a stew it
We knew that this would have to be

FERDY: Zulieka you're the one for me
what you decree, it have to be

BERNIE: Sybil I'll be good you'll see
I'll work hard and make you so happy

LENNIE: I'll swim the Thames for you Mary
Turn defeat to victory

DENNIS: I think I'm going to cry, Kathy,
Can this really happen to me?

FERDY: It's true
DENNIS: We want only you
LENNIE: What could we do
MEN: We're in love

WOMEN: You do it – We knew it
You blew it – We knew it
Who do it? – You do it
You undo it – You adieu it
You askew it – You kazoo it
Barbecue it – In a stew it
We knew that this would have to be

Song finishes.

FERDY: Zulieka –

ZULIEKA: Me and the girls have something to discuss. If you
would kindly wait outside.

FERDY, BERNIE, DENNIS and LENNIE exit.

MARY: We really going to keep them waiting for a year?

SYBIL: I don't think I can.

KATHY: No.

ZULIEKA: I know what you mean.

They laugh. The doorbell rings.

MARY: I'll go.

ZULIEKA: No.

Calling to the men.

Ferdy – Get the door, please.

FERDY: (*Voice off.*) Will do, my love.

KATHY: So when do we tell them?

SYBIL: Tomorrow?

ZULIEKA: Sure that's not too soon?

MARY: I don't think I can hold out much longer.

ZULIEKA: Truth be told – me neither.

FERDY re-enters. BERNIE, DENNIS and LENNIE follow him on. FERDY hands a telegram to ZULIEKA.

FERDY: Telegram.

ZULIEKA reads.

SYBIL: Zulieka...

KATHY: You okay?

ZULIEKA: My father has passed away.

FERDY: I'm so sorry.

MARY: If there's anything –

ZULIEKA: I'm all right.

Music cue.

ZULIEKA starts to clear away some cups and glasses. At first she seems in control, but suddenly she breaks down.

I don't even have the money to go to the funeral.

FERDY: We can lend you some.

ZULIEKA: You can't afford it.

MARY: We can club together.

ZULIEKA: I should have gone to him.

FERDY: You couldn't.

ZULIEKA: I let him down. He had so much faith in me.

FERDY: It's not your fault.

ZULIEKA: I was going to do such great things when I came here, and look at me.

FERDY: Don't blame yourself.

THE PRICE WE PAY (Reprise.)

FERDY: **For having hope**
ALL: **This is the price we pay**

FERDY: **For having dreams**
ALL: **This is the price we pay**

FERDY: **For having faith**
ALL: **This is the price we pay**

FERDY: **For having love**
ALL: **This is the price we pay**
This is the price we pay

Lights down.

Scene 9

Exterior: Piccadilly Circus.

Evening. ADMIRAL and JACQUELINE sitting on the steps of Eros. BERNIE and SYBIL, DENNIS and KATHY, LENNIE and MARY, FERDY and ZULIEKA, enter.

ADMIRAL: Hey, you out on the town?

FERDY: We have a night out. Before Zulieka go.

ADMIRAL: (*To ZULIEKA.*) I heard the news. Sorry.

ZULIEKA: You have a lot of questions to answer…

ADMIRAL: Just a lickle fun. So how long you will be away?

ZULIEKA: I can't be sure. Maybe a month. Maybe a year.

FERDY: A year?

ZULIEKA: It's impossible to say. You can wait that long can't you? You were meant to be giving up women for three years – remember?

FERDY: I remember.

Enter REVEREND.

REVEREND: (*To ZULIEKA.*) My sincere condolences.

ZULIEKA: Thank you, Reverend.

FERDY: I don't know if I can wait a whole year.

ADMIRAL: Don't look so glum.

FERDY: I can't help it.

108

ADMIRAL: Try to be positive.

It starts to snow.

DENNIS: Snow! It snowing! It snowing! It snowing!

ADMIRAL: Tell you what, I have a song...

LENNIE: Yeh man, we all heard your song.

ADMIRAL: No, no. I have a new song. Go like this...

BE GOOD TO YOURSELF

ADMIRAL: **When the one thing you really want**
You have to wait a while
And all your time must be well spent
With patience and a smile
When the rain is pouring down
And no one comes to call
Don't sit there on your fat backside
Just staring at the wall
When no one here will talk to you
Remind yourself what you must do
Be good to yourself – Look on the bright side
Don't get down – Stay on the right side
Don't get low – Don't let go
Don't let it show – Be good to yourself

ALL: **Be good to yourself – Look on the bright side**
Don't get down – Stay on the right side
Don't get low – Don't let go – Don't let it show
Be good to yourself

ADMIRAL: **When you are down and tired out**
Your life will make you shout
But in your head you must not doubt
Stay on the roundabout
When times get tough you're gonna need
Some flexibility
So stand up straight and take your time
There's no quick remedy
When you can't see a quick way through
Remind yourself what you must do

ALL: **Be good to yourself – Look on the bright side**
Don't get down – Stay on the right side

> Don't get low – Don't let go – Don't let it show
> Be good to yourself

ADMIRAL: **You will get a**
ALL: **Hard time**

ADMIRAL: **You will have a**
ALL: **Tough climb**

ADMIRAL: **Be accused of**
ALL: **All crime**
   In this city

ADMIRAL: **Love is hard in**
ALL: **Hard time**

ADMIRAL: **When you have a**
ALL: **Long climb**

ADMIRAL: **Looking for a**
ALL: **Good sign**
   In this city

ADMIRAL: **So...**

ALL: **Be good to yourself – Look on the bright side**
   Don't get down – Stay on the right side
   Don't get low – Don't let go – Don't let it show
   Be good to yourself

FERDY: That reminds me – I must amend our agreement.

ZULIEKA: Not now, Ferdy.

KATHY: Reverend, I was wondering if you would care to accompany Dennis and myself to the church hall this Saturday evening for a discussion on the subject of promiscuity.

REVEREND: I... Well, I... You see –

JACQUELINE: He's busy.

KATHY: Busy?

JACQUELINE: We're going ice-skating.

KATHY: Ice-skating?

REVEREND: We all need to let our hair down a little from time to time.

LENNIE: Amen!

KATHY: With a woman of easy virtue!

JACQUELINE: What did you say!

ZULIEKA: Enough! No arguments. Not today. Please.

KATHY: I apologise.

JACQUELINE: Apology accepted.

ZULIEKA: And Ferdy... What are you going to do while I'm away?

FERDY: Be good to myself.

ALL: **Be good to yourself – Look on the bright side**
Don't get down – Stay on the right side
Don't get low – Don't let go – Don't let it show
Be good to yourself
Be good to yourself
Be good to yourself

Song finishes. – Music cue.

LOVE STOP

ALL: **No more love**
Prohibition – Superstition – And attrition
I want love
Reclamation – Ministration – Orchestration
I want love
Revelation – Variation – Celebration
I want love
Ammunition – This admission – My ambition
I want love
With elation – In creation – My salvation
I want love
Information – No stagnation – Or vexation
No – Don't let the love stop
No – Never let the love stop
No – Don't let the love stop
No – Never let the love stop
No – Don't let the love stop
No – Never let the love stop
No – Don't let the love stop
No – Never let the love stop
Love stop!

111